# The Grumman X-29

Steve Pace

41

**TAB BOOKS**
Blue Ridge Summit, PA

This book is dedicated to the many past, present, and future X airplane pilots, for without their courageous efforts since 1946, America would not be at the forefront of aviation.

FIRST EDITION
FIRST PRINTING

© 1991 by Aero, an imprint of TAB BOOKS.
TAB BOOKS is a division of McGraw-Hill, Inc.

Library of Congress Cataloging-in-Publication Data

Pace, Steve.
    The Grumman X-29 / by Steve Pace.
        p.    cm. — (Aero series : v. 41)
    Includes bibliographical reference and index.
    ISBN 0-8306-3498-3 (pbk.)
    1. Grumman X-29A (Jet plane)   I. Title.
TL686.G78P33   1990
629.133′349—dc20                    90-1105
                                      CIP

TAB BOOKS offers software for sale. For information and a catalog, please contact
TAB Software Department, Blue Ridge Summit, PA 17294-0850.

Questions regarding the content of this book
should be addressed to:

    Reader Inquiry Branch
    TAB BOOKS
    Blue Ridge Summit, PA 17294

Acquisitions Editor: Jeff Worsinger
Book Editor: Steven H. Mesner
Production: Katherine G. Brown
Series Design: Jaclyn J. Boone

Front cover: photograph courtesy of Grumman via Ted Wierzbanowski.
Back cover: photograph courtesy of NASA via Ted Wierzbanowski.

# Contents

# Foreword

WHEN I checked in with the AFFTC X-29A Program Office at Edwards AFB, I was greeted with: "Welcome to the X-29A program. You'll be our next (second) Air Force Flight Test Center X-29A Program Manager and Test Pilot. At this time we don't have time to give you a dedicated sortie for training. We're just going to go for it. Get as much simulator and cockpit time as you want and let us know when you'll be ready. Your first flight will be an envelope expansion to 1.10 Mach at 30,000 feet." So much for in-flight training time before the biggest flight of my life. I was told: "Go ahead and feel the airplane out as you climb to 30,000 feet, but fuel is critical so don't take too much time. We need to hit the data points so we can get on with envelope expansion." I knew at that point that this program would be unlike any program I'd been on before.

The X-29A program was a great step forward for the experimental aircraft community. We hadn't flown a new X aircraft in 10 years and the push to get the X-29 into the air was a benefit to the entire aerospace community. Experimental aircraft programs need to be an ongoing effort to allow experimenters the opportunity to investigate what the paper concepts will do in real life. The role of experimental aircraft in the evolution of flight is often misunderstood or undervalued. For relatively low cost, we can develop and validate, in-flight, key technologies for future use. X aircraft are win-win situations—if you find that the technology isn't ready for production or viable at all, you still come out ahead because (to paraphrase Mr. Edison), "failed experiments tell us what not to do."

The X-29A program is a unique and wonderful program. It allows us to look into numerous aircraft technologies and flight test methodologies that can and will be used in the future. The techniques developed and refined during X-29 flight testing give the aerospace community new and refined tools for data acquisition and evaluation. The technologies on the X-29 can be used to reduce total drag as well as enhance future fighter maneuverability.

People wonder why the forward-swept wing

works and why we should build this type of aircraft. The answer is: "Why not?" In the past, we were restricted to aft-swept wings due to material constraints. With improved materials—in this case, advanced composite materials—we are able to build a wing that can be "tuned" to do the job and still provide adequate strength-to-weight margin. The benefit is reduced drag in the transonic speed regime. Drag reduction is a hard thing to nail down due to the numerous contributors to total drag, but in the case of the X-29, the net reduction in drag due to lift when compared to an aft swept wing is considerable—20 to 40 percent. This degree of performance increase can easily be translated into improved fighter performance and maneuverability. As you will see in the text, forward-swept wings go back to the earliest supersonic designs. It is just now that we have the technology to build and fly them in the supersonic speed regime. We had been strapped to the subsonic speed regime prior to the advent of the X-29A.

The other major technologies in the X-29 were included in the test program to complement the forward swept wing. These made the X-29 possible and, at the same time, allowed the program to explore a multifaceted problem. The variable camber, three-surface lift, and full authority close-coupled canard are all technologies that can—and I think *should*—be incorporated into future fighter designs.

I've often been asked how it feels to fly an airplane that relies on a computer to "stay in the air." It feels just like any other modern fighter. The state of aerodynamic stability and control allows us to now employ a central processor to enhance the control of the air vehicle. In other words, the computer in the X-29A is there to help the pilot get more out of the aircraft. Similar advances have occurred in the past. We went from wing warping to ailerons, added hydraulic boosting of flying control surfaces, and then went to a hydromechanical control surface. And at each step along the way, these advances gave the pilot more precise and absolute control over the aircraft. The addition of a computer is nothing more than an evolutionary step in the process of gaining control over the aircraft. Digital flight control systems are here to stay and will enable us to extract more performance and control from our aircraft.

My few flights in the number one X-29A were a wonderful experience. I was privileged to work with all the members of the test team from the Air Force, NASA, and Grumman. It is rare in this day to have the opportunity to do envelope expansion and performance testing on a new aircraft. The X-29 performs well and has very few maintenance problems. Our major problems stemmed from instrumentation and the desire to gather large amounts of data on each sortie—the aircraft is indeed a flying laboratory. Overall, X-29 performance can be equated to

*Fig. I-1.*

an F-16, but with the caveat that it is a one-of-a-kind experimental aircraft and not a missionized production fighter. There are no weapon systems nor avionics. The handling qualities improved over the span of my 33 flights to the point that they were adequate for the research role but were not optimized for a frontline fighter. The recent changes to the control laws that have enabled flights of the number two airplane in excess of 50 degrees angle of attack have significantly improved the handling qualities and have made the X-29A even more fun to fly.

When I was selected to become the second X-29 Air Force pilot, I was elated. It was an opportunity for me to contribute to the aerospace community and to be a part of the next generation of fighter technology. I hope I served my peers well and thank the Lord for the opportunity to contribute in my small way.

There is no way I can close without giving my lasting appreciation (and that of my wife and kids) to the crew chief and maintenance folks who kept the airplane safe and ready to fly. They were kind enough to let me take their precious X plane out of the hangar and fly it occasionally. The real heros of the X-29A test program, however, are the numerous engineers from the Air Force, NASA, and Grumman who dedicated themselves (and are still doing so) to the monumental effort of gathering and analyzing the wealth of information obtained from the X-29. My heartfelt thanks to all.

Lt. Col. Harry C. Walker III
Chief, Special Projects Division,
USAF Test Pilot School
(former AFFTC X-29A Program Manager
and Test Pilot)
March 16, 1990

# Acknowledgments

I WOULD like to give my most sincere thanks to the following airframe and powerplant contractors and government bodies for providing the graphics for this volume of the Aero Series: Grumman Corporation, General Electric Company, Rockwell International Corporation, General Dynamics Corporation, United States Air Force, and National Aeronautics and Space Administration.

I would also like to relay my thanks to the following individuals who assisted me with graphics and information research: Lois Lovisolo, Corporate Historian, Grumman Corporation; Peter E. Kirkup, Assistant Historian/Public Affairs, Grumman Corporation; Z. Joe Thornton, Manager, Public Affairs, General Dynamics; Mike Mathews, Director, Public Relations, Rockwell International; William C. (Chris) Wamsley, Supervisor, Photo Laboratory, Rockwell International; Erik Simonsen, Public Relations, Rockwell International; Erik Simonsen, Freelance Photography; Nancy Lovato, Public Affairs Officer, NASA; Don Haley, Public Affairs Officer, NASA; Laurel Mann, X-29 Project Secretary, NASA; Cheryl Gumm, Archivist, Office of History, HQ/AFFTC; Lt. Col. Ted Wierzbanowski, ex-AFFTC X-29A Program Manager/Test Pilot; Maj. Bud Jenschke, 6510 TW, Edwards AFB; Les Reinertson, Public Affairs Officer, NASA; Col. Dave McCloud, ex-Director of Advanced Programs for TAC; Randy (Mr. Scratchbuild) Cannon, a special friend; Jo Anne Rumple, Public Affairs Office, HQ/ASD; Lt. Col. Jeff Riemer, USAF; Col. John Hoffman, Vice Commander, HQ/AFFTC; Robert Salvucci, Public Relations, General Electric; Lt. Col. Harry Walker, ex-AFFTC X-29A Program Manager/Test Pilot; Mike Wallace, Public Affairs Office, HQ/ASD; Gary Trippensee, NASA X-29A Project Manager; and the editorial staff at TAB BOOKS.

# Introduction

THE GRUMMAN X-29A Forward-Swept Wing Advanced Technology Demonstrator program represents a concerted effort toward future development of more advanced aircraft by the United States Air Force (USAF), Defense Advanced Research Projects Agency (DARPA), National Aeronautics and Space Administration (NASA), and a multitude of aerospace entities nationwide. Development of the X-29 aircraft was derived from speeded-up investigations and technology validation studies to create a viable forward-swept-wing air vehicle capable of not only subsonic speed as before, but of transonic and supersonic speeds as well. This has been accomplished.

From the outset, the X-29 program had three primary objectives. The first was to prove the benefits of the forward-swept wing and its related technologies in flight; the second was to confirm the airworthiness of the advanced technology demonstrator aircraft within an adequate angle-of-attack and speed and altitude envelope; the third was to transfer program results to government and industry in a timely manner. How X-29 elements function in an integrated system will provide answers that may change the way next-generation aircraft, are designed. A tremendous amount of data has been accumulated already, with much more to come. It will take years to process these data.

Grumman's X-29 program is sponsored by DARPA, a special agency within the Department of Defense (DoD) chartered to develop high-risk technologies with potentially high benefits. The flight demonstrator program is administered by the Air Force Flight Dynamics Laboratory (AFFDL), Wright-Patterson AFB, Ohio. Flight testing is carried out by NASA's Ames-Dryden Flight Research Facility (ADFRF), Edwards AFB, California, and data released through it, the Air Force, and Grumman flight test reports.

Grumman Corporation, Bethpage, New York, is the prime contractor for the X-29 program. The two X-29A aircraft were assembled at the company's Product Development Center (PDC) at Bethpage.

First flown in late 1984, the number one X-29A ended its two-phase, four-year flight test program in late 1988; it flew 242 times and accumulated 178.6 flight hours. When it flew its 200th test hop, it set a record for X-type aircraft, surpassing the 199 flights flown by the X-15 air vehicles. Thus the X-29 became the safest X airplane ever flown, never having experienced a crash or a major mishap.

First flown in mid-1989, the number two X-29A is optimized for a high alpha (high angle of attack) flight test program. To investigate the maximum ability of the forward-swept wing, the number two X-29A is expected to fly some 70 flights, and up to a 70-degree angle of attack without any serious side effects.

Fighter-like, the X-29A aircraft are well-liked by their assigned and guest pilots. Flying on a rotational basis, X-29 pilots look forward to their next turn. It has proved to be very responsive, maneuverable and forgiving—a pilot's dream. It is a trend-setter, an unorthodox airplane that performs better than was expected.

# 1

# Historical Overview

BIRDS HAVE been flying since prehistoric time, when pterodactyls roamed the skies above a much younger Earth. The human race did not match that extinct flying reptile's accomplishment until the year 1903, when mankind itself began to fly somewhat like the avian we know today.

But in our never ending quest to find better and safer ways to fly, mankind must continue to improve upon the four major parameters that are associated with manned flight—aeronautics, aerodynamics, powerplants, and airframes.

Indeed, mankind has learned a great deal about flight in a relatively short period of time. We have flown some 25 times the speed of sound and to and from the moon nine times. Back here on planet Earth, however, where an atmosphere exists, we are forced to cope with its penalizing reality, and continue to refine our newfound flying prowess—not like the avian, like the human, for we have not stagnated.

Too often, advancements in the aforementioned parameters of flight appear to be in a holding pattern—too few, and too far apart. But when an advancement is discovered, developed, and ultimately put to flight test, manned flight can—and often does—improve dramatically.

The first major element of flight, aeronautics, is the actual design and construction of aircraft—past, present, and future. It is the most basic parameter of manned flight.

The second entity, aerodynamics, is the science that deals with the motion of gases and especially with the atmospheric forces exerted on aircraft. This part of manned flight improves range and endurance, and speed and maneuverability by reducing the penalties imposed on aircraft by drag.

The third ingredient, the powerplant, is the primary propulsion unit or units that propel aircraft, whether piston, turbojet, fanjet, or rocket power, or any combination thereof.

The fourth major component, the airframe, is the complete interior and exterior structure of aircraft. Aircraft airframes have evolved from wood-and-fabric to metal alloys such as aluminum, stainless steel, and titanium.

Now comes a relatively new fifth major parameter of manned flight, a breakthrough in airframe construction that already has improved manned flight, and will continue to do so. It is called construction with advanced composite materials.

## Advanced Composite Materials

Advanced composite materials, applied to aircraft in various ways, are rapidly replacing metallic alloys in aircraft construction, much as the latter replaced wood-and-fabric aircraft construction, as the monoplane replaced the biplane, as the jet age replaced the piston age.

Advanced composite materials such as Fibaloy, carbon-carbon, boron, Kevlar (pound per pound, five times stronger than steel), graphite or carbon fibers, and thermoplastics are some composite materials that are not only lighter and stronger than most metallic alloys employed in aircraft airframes, they withstand greater temperatures and absorb radar. In other words, they are to aeronautical engineers what Voyager 2 has been to Earth-bound astronomers—priceless.

With the five major parameters working in concert now—aeronautics, aerodynamics, powerplants, airframes, and advanced composite materials—some early aircraft design ideas that were once shelved are now reappearing. One in particular is the forward-swept wing (FSW).

## Forward-Swept Wing

The forward-swept wing is a relatively new wing planform that reduces drag up to 20 percent in the transonic speed maneuvering range (600 to 800 or Mach .8 to 1.2), giving lower-powered aircraft the same performance as higher-powered aircraft, thus saving weight and reducing size. The FSW concept is not a new one, as it has been around since the early days of wood-and-fabric airframes. But using advanced composite materials in the construction of aircraft is a new design philosophy.

German designers used a forward-swept wing concept during World War II to manufacture a four-jet bomber airplane, the Junkers Ju-287 (FIG. 1-1). Junkers developed this bomber with a 20-degree forward-swept wing planform in an effort to increase bomb bay area. Configured this way, the Ju-287 would have been able to transport one large bomb on its CG (center of gravity), and its FSW was intended to eliminate the need for trim change after the heavy bomb was released. Junkers successfully flight-tested its FSW Ju-287 bomber prototype 17 times before it was captured by the Russians in 1944. (By that time it had been damaged during Allied bombing raids and it is believed that it never flew again.) The Ju-287 had demonstrated good low-speed control during its short-lived career, but it also showed a possible high-speed problem called *structural divergence*. In other words, its FSW had a tendency to twist, an aerodynamic problem that could have ripped the wings from the fuselage at the roots if the divergent speed had been attained or exceeded. This structural divergence problem was very serious, and caused the FSW concept to be abandoned again until the early 1960s, when the Hamburger Flugzeugbau (HFB) 320 Hansa business jet was introduced in Germany (FIG. 1-2).

In its effort to allow a full-height passenger cabin, HFB made 50 twin-jet Hansa bizjets with metal FSWs located aft of the pressurized passenger compartment. These aircraft were engineered specifically for additional passenger comfort, not for

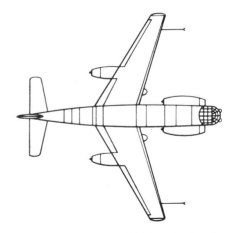

*Fig. 1-1. The Junkers Ju-287 four-jet bomber with its 20-degree FSW planform.* Grumman Corporation

2

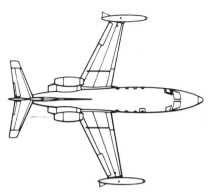

*Fig.1-2. HFB-320 Hansajet twin-jet business jet with its 15-degree FSW.* Grumman Corporation

high-speed transportation. Their wings, like those of the Ju-287, are swept forward (15 degrees), and no serious structural problems surfaced within their designated flight envelope.

Earlier forward-swept wing designs such as the Cornelius XFG-1 fuel-carrying glider (two built), a Bell X-1 derivative with FSW (wind tunnel model), a Douglas D-558 Skystreak variant with FSW (a paper airplane), a Russian FSW glider design by V. P. Tsibin, and even an FSW version of the North American P-51 Mustang went nowhere. The designers and manufacturers of these aircraft fully realized their wings would have to be very heavy to provide the strength required to eliminate structural divergence during high-speed flight. Therefore, because a practical FSW concept didn't exist, aerodynamicists frowned upon their use in the design of aircraft.

## Inventing a Practical Forward-Swept Wing

Inventing a practical forward-swept wing was a major goal of retired U.S. Air Force Colonel Norris J. Krone, Jr. He was, in fact, obsessed with the idea.

Krone, already holding bachelor's and master's degrees in aeronautical engineering, studied for his Ph.D. in aeronautical engineering, during which time he academically researched the FSW concept and found it to be an old philosophy of design, in that a number of aircraft had been designed and/or built to employ the FSW planform. Further, with few exceptions, Krone found that none of them were optimized for high-speed flight, that most of them had been designed for low-speed flight.

This discovery increased his interest and he pursued his FSW idea, setting his sights on advanced aircraft that would be able to maneuver safely through all speed ranges. Krone's thesis is entitled *Divergence Elimination with Advanced Composites*, and it explains how, by use of advanced composite materials with aeroelastic tailoring, a practical forward-swept wing could be built and flown on high-performance aircraft.

After Krone got his Ph.D. in 1974, he went to work for the DARPA (Defense Advanced Research Projects Agency), a special branch of the DoD (Department of Defense) chartered to develop high-risk aerospace technologies with potentially high benefits, in 1976 at Arlington, Virginia. He subsequently managed a number of advanced aircraft design projects, including the creation of a practical high-energy FSW aircraft.

The DARPA, because of its unique position within the Government, was able to release an RFP (request for proposal) in 1976 for the development of a manned FSW technology demonstrator airplane, one able to go beyond subsonic speed—safely—without tearing its wings off its fuselage. As required, its wings would be made of aeroelastically-tailored advanced composite material, specifically, from graphite (carbon fiber) mixed with epoxy resins and cured in an autoclave.

DARPA then, with the assistance of the Air Force Flight Dynamics Laboratory (AFFDL) division of the Aeronautical Systems Division (ASD) of the Air Force and NASA (National Aeronautics and Space Administration), awarded study contracts to three qualifying airframe contractors in June of 1977—General Dynamics Corporation, Grumman Corporation, and Rockwell International Corporation. This trio, slowly funded because of budget cuts during the Carter administration, participated in a series of feasibility studies and wind tunnel model investigations during the period 1977–81.

The three airframe contractors delivered their respective forward-swept wing aircraft proposals in 1981. After consideration of these designs, Grumman's was judged best. It was felt that Grumman's FSW design would better serve the evaluation of a manned, flying forward-swept wing technology

3

demonstrator. A contract for two aircraft was delivered to Grumman so it could carry on.

Grumman's proposed FSW aircraft, Design G-712, was designated X-29A in September 1981 and its first flight date was scheduled for mid-1983. What promised to be a highly maneuverable X airplane, the X-29, had emerged from an old concept—a concept revived and made practical by Norris Krone. It was his work that had turned the key to unlock the FSW's basic problem of structural instability. Now, a forward-swept wing aircraft would fly again. This time, it would not be limited to subsonic speed, but allowed to fly at any speed its creators allowed.

### Proposals

The FSW aircraft proposals were similar, due to their respective FSW planforms, yet quite different. They are described below:

*General Dynamics Corporation.* General Dynamics of Fort Worth, Texas, proposed a modified version of its highly successful F-16 Fighting Falcon, which it designated SFW/F-16 (Swept Forward Wing F-16, FIG. 1-3). It appeared to be a factory-type F-16A model with FSW and no canard foreplanes, albeit these might have been required later. It is interesting to note that their design showed retention of the F-16's basic armament (two wingtip-mounted AIM-9 Sidewinder air-to-air missiles and a single 20mm cannon). The SFW/F-16 was to employ the existing fuselage, cockpit and canopy, vertical tail, stabilator, ventral strakes, ventral engine air inlet, and ducting, in addition to the same Pratt & Whitney F100-PW-200 engine of production F-16A/B model aircraft, with a new forward-swept wing in place of the usual F-16 aft-swept wing. General Dynamics' plan was to quickly provide a manned FSW technology demonstrator that would provide data to help determine the actual design of the FSW made from aeroelastically-tailored advanced composite material.

*Grumman Corporation.* Grumman Corporation of Bethpage, New York, proposed a composite aircraft made up of key parts from other aircraft to

*Fig. 1-3. The proposed General Dynamics SFW/F-16.*

General Dynamics Corporation

4

*Fig. 1-4. The Grumman X-29A FSW technology demonstrator is shown in its final configuration.*

save development time and money. This plan eventually won the competition for them. Grumman's design borrowed the entire nose section from the Northrop F-5A Freedom Fighter; the main landing gear, hydraulic actuators, jet fuel starter and emergency power unit from the F-16; F-5A nose landing gear, cockpit, canopy, and environmental control system; Martin-Baker Model IRQ7A zero-zero (zero speed-zero altitude) ejection seat; Grumman EA-6B Prowler hydraulic fluid reservoirs; and the 16,000-pound thrust class General Electric F404-GE-400 augmented (afterburning) fanjet engine employed by the McDonnell Douglas F/A-18 Hornet and other aircraft. The new parts of this hybrid aircraft would be its mid and aft fuselage sections, vertical tail, canard foreplanes—and, of course, its forward-swept wing. Strakes were added to the F-5A's nose radome cone (on a horizontal plane) in an effort to prevent the instability characteristics of the F-5A at very high angles of attack (above 35 degrees). Figure 1-4 shows the final Grumman X-29A configuration; Figure 1-5 the composite makeup of the airplane.

*Rockwell International Corporation.* Rockwell's North American Aircraft of Los Angeles, California, offered up a brand new design with FSW and aftward swept canard foreplanes which it designated X-FSW (eXperimental-Forward Swept Wing) and dubbed Sabrebat. A very realistic full-scale mockup was constructed out of styrofoam to show its FSW design (FIG. 1-6). The Sabrebat was to be 51 feet long, 12.25 feet high, and span 29.54 feet. Like Grumman's FSW design, it would use a single F404 fanjet engine for power; however, it featured a ventral engine air inlet and ducting system *a la* F-16, while Grumman's design incorporated cheek-type engine air inlets of the fixed geometry type. Rockwell's Sabrebat showed ventral strakes and the use of wingtip-mounted missiles and a single cannon, but its most noticeable feature was its very large bubble-type cockpit canopy for 360-degree pilot visibility (FIG. 1-7). Although Rockwell's proposed X-FSW Sabrebat was unique, it was Grumman's FSW design that became the X-29A.

At first glance, the Grumman X-29A FSW technology demonstrator looks to be flying backwards (FIG. 1-8). Its sharply forward-swept wings are mounted far back on the fuselage, while its canard foreplanes (horizontal stabilators for pitch control) are mounted in front of the main wings instead of behind them. The X-29 uses a close-coupled design that places the canard foreplanes close to, and in the same plane as, the FSWs. The complex geometries of the FSW and canards work in concert to give the airplane its exceptional maneuverability, unprecedented transonic performance, high lift and low drag, and light airframe structure. Using the respon-

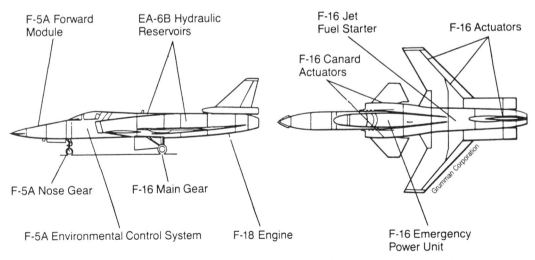

*Fig. 1-5. Off-the-shelf components employed by the Grumman X-29A are shown.*

**Fig. 1-6.** *The full-scale styrofoam mockup of the Rockwell X-FSW Sabrebat proposal.*

**Fig. 1-7.** *The excellent visibility potential of Rockwell's proposed Sabrebat is shown here.*

*Fig. 1-8. At first glance, the Grumman X-29A appears to be flying backwards.*

sive F404 fanjet engine, already classed as a hallmark, the X-29 has showed its advanced technologies successfully. These technologies will allow future aircraft to fly faster and farther with less power.

By flying the FSW X-29 airplane right off the drawing board, its proof of concepts might—and most likely will—seriously alter the thinking of future aircraft designers. It performs more efficiently over a wider range of speeds than aircraft with aft-swept wings, meaning more lift and less drag (thus a greater lift-to-drag ratio), superior maneuverability and agility, and more efficient cruise speed to decrease fuel consumption and increase range end endurance.

The number two X-29A is in the skies over Edwards AFB. It and its sister ship may prove to be the springboard for a new generation of highly agile, lightweight fighter-type aircraft that are more fuel efficient, with better sustained performance and available at much lower cost—the last factor looming ever more critical as new combat aircraft grow progressively more sophisticated and costly (witness Northrop's B-2 Advanced Technology Bomber).

The Grumman X-29A represents, a concerted responsibility to future aircraft development by the aerospace industries for the U.S. armed forces. It is the X-29 that is leading the way.

# 2

# Developmental Highlights

DEVELOPMENT of the Grumman X-29A FSW technology demonstrator aircraft traces back to the year 1975, when Rockwell earned the right to build a pair of subscale RPRVs (remotely piloted research vehicles) under a joint USAF/NASA program called the HiMAT (Highly Maneuverable Aircraft Technology) program. The HiMAT program was optimized to investigate the interrelated problems of all aspects of flight of a typical advanced fighter configuration. The program was also to contribute to the design of future fighter types by furnishing fundamental aerodynamic and structural loads data that would assist future combat aircraft designers (FIG. 2-1).

The HiMAT air vehicle's basic concept was that of a close-coupled canard foreplane layout, with advanced composite material airfoil design with aeroelastic tailoring. It was a subscale model of an advanced fighter, synthesized by Rockwell designers as typical in the year 1990. Powered by a single afterburning General Electric J85-GE-21 turbojet

engine, these air vehicles were capable of Mach 1.6 speed and 45 minutes duration. They had a launch weight of 3,500 pounds, body diameter of 2.7 feet, wingspan of 15.6 feet, and length of 23.6 feet.

A relatively new trend at the time, advanced composite materials accounted for nearly one-third of the airframe structural weight of the HiMAT air vehicles, and for the first time, these materials were being used to capitalize on their ability to give unidirectional stiffness. The composite wing and canard flying surfaces were designed so both the natural bending of both surfaces under maneuvering loads would control the changing of the air vehicles to maintain optimum lift and drag conditions. The HiMAT air vehicles were air-launched from a B-52 mothership (FIG. 2-2) and flown by pilots on the ground via digital remote control in a special control room. These unmanned air vehicles were capable of extremely high-G maneuvers without tearing apart—up to 18G or about twice that of manned aircraft.

*Fig. 2-1. Rockwell's HiMAT, Model NR-870, at its rollout.*

### Loss of the HiMAT Competition

After they lost the HiMAT competition, which it had fought hard to win, Grumman set out to find out why. Under the guidance of Glenn L. Spacht (FIG. 2-3), Grumman's HiMAT project engineer, Grumman authorized a company-funded wind tunnel test program, using its conventionally configured aft-swept-wing design as a baseline model (FIG. 2-4). The idea was to find out exactly why their HiMAT proposal was not accepted. These wind tunnel investigations were run at NASA's Langley Research Center, Hampton, Virginia.

Ironically, Col. Krone was working at NASA Langley at the time. Thus he quickly became aware

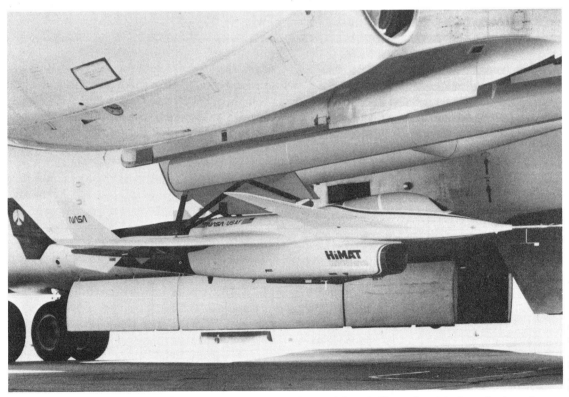

*Fig. 2-2. Rockwell's HiMAT under the starboard wing of its B-52 mothership launch aircraft.*

Fig. 2-3. Glenn L. Spacht.

*Fig. 2-4. Artist's conception of Grumman's proposed HiMAT RPRV configuration, but shown as a full-scale, manned aircraft for clarity. Note its variable-geometry swing-wing planform like that of the F-14 Tomcat.*

of Grumman's HiMAT follow-on program and became very familiar with it, Glenn Spacht, and Spacht's team. He also felt strongly that he had the cure for Grumman's HiMAT ailment. Krone suggested that Grumman's wing root problem, which was being experienced by the wind tunnel model, could be eliminated by installing forward-swept wings. He insisted that by combining construction with advanced composite material (being used) with aeroelastic tailoring (being used), a forward swept wing would work, and it would be light, strong, and divergence-proof. Grumman followed his lead and installed forward-swept wings on its wind tunnel model (FIG. 2-5).

Krone's suggestion proved out, and after Grumman's wind tunnel program ended a few weeks later, Grumman decided to move forward with the idea of actually developing a full-scale, manned, HiMAT-type aircraft with aeroelastically-tailored advanced composite material forward-swept wings with close-coupled canard foreplanes, optimized for all speed ranges—unheard of with such a wing planform. Spacht was appointed deputy program director for development. It was a bold move on Grumman's part, especially since it had to use in-house monies.

### Actual Development

Actual development of what would become the Grumman X-29A began when the preliminary design team with Grumman's Advanced Aircraft Systems Department came up with a workable forward-swept wing design.

To test its design without spending a great deal

*Fig. 2-5. Early FSW wind tunnel model that was tested by Grumman with its own monies.*

of monies, an RC (radio-controlled) model airplane of balsa wood, featuring canards (foreplanes) and a forward-swept wing that spanned seven feet was built. Powered by a 2 1/2 horsepower glow-plug model airplane engine housed within its fuselage, driving a ducted propeller (fan, if you will), the model was propelled by air thrust out its tail, much like a jet engine. The model could be made to stall (lose all lift), but it would not spin. Subsequently, a more elaborate wind tunnel model was built that underwent many hours of supersonic wind tunnel evaluation, up to a speed of Mach 1.5, successfully (FIG. 2-6). More importantly, it demonstrated excellent transonic capability. Grumman was now solidly behind their venture.

Col. Krone had joined the DARPA organization by this time, and with his existing FSW interest and timely persuasion, feasibility study contracts for the ultimate development of a full-scale manned FSW technology demonstrator aircraft went out to the aforementioned trio of airframe contractors. Of course, Grumman had a head start. It was now 1977, and the three airframe contractors moved forward with the development of their respective FSW aircraft proposals, to be submitted for evaluation in 1981.

Grumman was able to freeze its preliminary FSW design (G-712) in early 1979 and initiate its Phase One development program in July of that same year. Their Phase One effort focused on analytical and empirical workings to assess the critical technology issues such as the type of airfoil shape (cross section), flight control system, and so on. A series of wind tunnel tests, advanced composite material(s) evaluations and ways to process them ensued. Manned and unmanned simulations resolved these issues prior to the start of Phase Two.

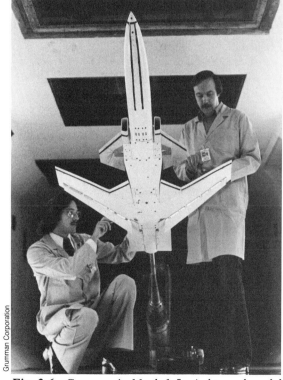

*Fig. 2-6. Grumman's Mach 1.5 wind tunnel model of its proposed FSW aircraft.*

Grumman began Phase Two in January of 1981. This phase consisted of detail design, fabrication, and ground and flight tests of the craft—if in fact Grumman got the nod to actually produce the FSW airplane.

After detailed studies of all entries, it was announced on 22 December 1981 that Grumman had won the competition and would build two FSW technology demonstrator aircraft. A $71.3 million contract followed.

Because the airplane would not be a prototype of an actual combat type, but rather a pure experimental aircraft, the designation X-29A was given. Therefore, it would follow the 28 X-types that had been built or proposed before it. The serial numbers 82-0003 and 82-0049 were issued to X-29A number one and two respectively. Actual construction of X-29A number one began in January of 1982; its first flight was rescheduled for April of 1984 (originally slated for mid-1983), but this date was to slip also.

It had been decided earlier that no matter which contractor won the FSW aircraft competition, that contractor would perform the initial CEFs (contractor evaluation flights) prior to any government flight test activities. The CEFs would be flights one through four.

Grumman's Flight Test Department, headed by Grumman's Chief Test Pilot Charles A. (Chuck) Sewell, needed to select its X-29A project pilot and co-project pilot. Sewell selected himself as the former, and Grumman test pilot Kurt C. Schroeder as the latter. NASA chose Stephen D. (Steve) Ishmael to serve as its X-29A project pilot, and Rogers E. Smith as its X-29A co-project pilot. The USAF selected Lt. Col. Theodore J. (Ted) Wierzbanowski to be its AFFTC (Air Force Flight Test Center) X-29A program manager and test pilot. These five assigned X-29A pilots would be responsible for making or breaking the X-29A FSW technology demonstrator—the first X airplane in 10 years.

## Birth of the X-29A

The birth of the X-29A occurred on 27 August 1984 at Grumman's Calverton, New York, facility on Long Island. Because X-29A number two had been painted before number one, it was used in the official rollout ceremony. Figure 2-7 shows X-29A number two after the rollout ceremony.

Grumman Corporation President George M. Skurla pointed out that the introduction of the X-29A was a very proud day for the company. He said, ''It is a significant milestone in Grumman's history and further evidence of our continuing commitment to expand the frontiers of manned flight. The X-29 is a means to investigate, in flight, new technologies that could point the way toward future generations of aircraft which are more agile, burn less fuel, and cost less to maintain than any tactical aircraft flying today.''

Grumman Corporation Chairman John C. Bierwirth noted that Grumman has made a long-term commitment to the development of high technologies that its customers require. ''The X-29 is a

*Fig. 2-7. X-29A number two as it appeared shortly after its rollout ceremony.*

product of that commitment,'' Bierwirth said. ''For Grumman it represents a very substantial investment of funds, an investment of personal dedication, and an investment of Grumman pride.''

Following the rollout ceremony, X-29A number two was placed in storage at Calverton to await funding for its flight test program. The program focus then shifted toward X-29A number one.

Before any new aircraft type can begin its flight test program(s), it must first undergo a series of low- and high-speed taxis to check steering, brakes, etc. This important preflight stage for the first X-29A example began the day after number two rolled out. Unpainted, with Grumman's Chuck Sewell at its throttle, X-29A-1 performed five progressive low-speed taxi runs at Calverton in increments of 10 knots, beginning at 20 and ending at 60 knots (FIGS. 2-8 and 2-9). Everything in its low-speed taxi range checked out. Because no accidental liftoff was desired (possibly ending with unwanted flight at this restricted location for X-type aircraft), the high-speed taxis to estimated rotation speed for takeoff were deferred as planned. These would take place later at the NASA Ames-Dryden Flight Research Facility at Edwards AFB, California, where all flight testing of the X-29A FSW technology demonstrator aircraft would be conducted.

In September 1984, X-29A number one was stripped of its F404 engine, painted exactly like X-29A number two, then wrapped in a protective blanket for its ocean voyage to California. To begin its journey, it was trucked to Port Jefferson from Calverton on 21 September, loaded on a barge (FIG. 2-10), and floated to Bayonne, New York. There it was loaded on a government ship for its ocean cruise to San Pedro, California, via the Panama Canal. After the plane arrived at San Pedro, it was again loaded on an 18-wheeler and trucked overland to Edwards. It arrived there on 11 October (FIG. 2-11). The engine was reinstalled, and the exotic airplane was prepared for its high-speed taxis and subsequent CEFs.

At Edwards now, with Sewell under glass, X-29A number one began its series of high-speed taxi runs on 4 December 1984 (FIG. 2-12). Eight runs had been planned for that day, but low hydraulic fluid pressure in the aircraft's EPU (emergency power unit) ended the day after high-speed taxi number six. The EPU was fixed overnight and two more runs were made on the following day. One run, to 134 knots, caused a brief liftoff, which Sewell ended by immediately cutting engine power. Upon his return to the flight operations office, he said the airplane was now ready for flight. The premier flight was then scheduled for 10 December, but Mother Nature was not having any part of it.

Grumman Corporation

*Fig. 2-8. X-29A-1 during its 60-knot low-speed taxi run.*

*Fig. 2-9. X-29A-1 slowing after a low-speed taxi run at Calverton.*

*Fig. 2-10. X-29A-1 being loaded on a barge at Port Jefferson.*

NASA

*Fig. 2-11. X-29A-1 after its arrival at Edwards.*

Grumman Corporation

*Fig. 2-12. X-29A-1 taxiing out for high-speed taxi runs at Edwards.*

# 3

# Technologies, Systems, and Configuration

GRUMMAN X-29A aircraft feature a number of advanced technologies and systems in a unique configuration (FIGS. 3-1 and 3-2). It is for this reason the X-29 is called an advanced technology demonstrator. Its most prominent feature is, of course, its forward-swept wing.

### Forward-Swept Wing

The forward-swept wing (or FSW) planform of the X-29A aircraft could—and probably will—change the way future aircraft designers pattern wing planforms for advanced tactical aircraft, much as the aft-swept wing (ASW) did for aircraft designers in the past (FIG. 3-3), because now, with its aeroelastically-tailored advanced composite material construction, the FSW works.

The forward-swept wing of the X-29A aircraft has already made its mark, performing more efficiently over the entire speed spectrum—subsonic, transonic (especially), and supersonic—than aircraft with ASWs (FIG. 3-4). This means that the X-29 has more lift, less drag, exceptional maneuverability and agility, and more efficient cruise speed for improved fuel enconomy and mission endurance.

During flight, air moving over the forward-swept wing of the X-29 flows inward toward the root of the wing instead of outward toward the tip, as it does on aircraft with aft-swept wings (FIG. 3-5). This *reversed air flow*, as it is called, allows the wingtips, with their ailerons, to remain unstalled at high angles of attack (FIG. 3-6). Stall, or loss of lift, that does occur develops at the root of the forward-swept wing, where it is easier to control. Because of this factor, the X-29 is more responsive to low speed and high AOA (angle of attack) maneuvering than aircraft with aft-swept wings.

The performance of the FSW when compared to that of an ASW results in drag reductions of up to 20 percent, and as high as 45 percent, in the transonic speed range. This gives the X-29 the same performance as an aircraft with a much more powerful engine. While the X-29 uses a 16,000-pound

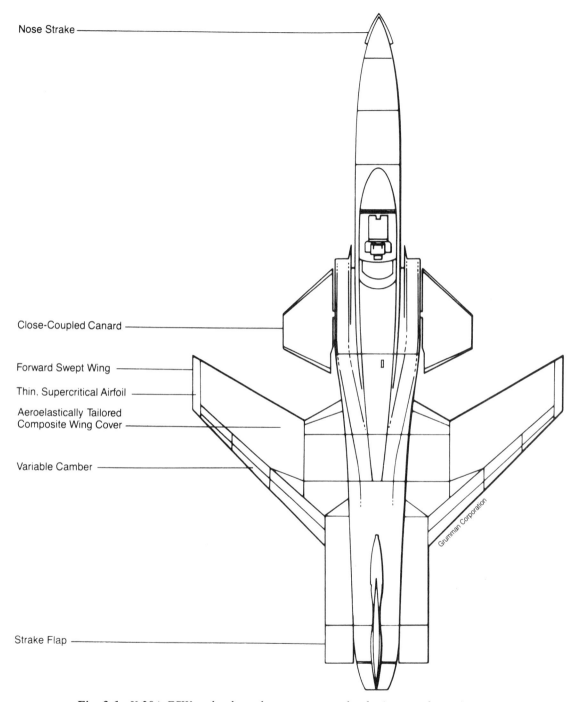

Nose Strake

Close-Coupled Canard

Forward Swept Wing

Thin. Supercritical Airfoil

Aeroelastically Tailored
Composite Wing Cover

Variable Camber

Strake Flap

Grumman Corporation

*Fig. 3-1. X-29A FSW technology demonstrator technologies are shown in part.*

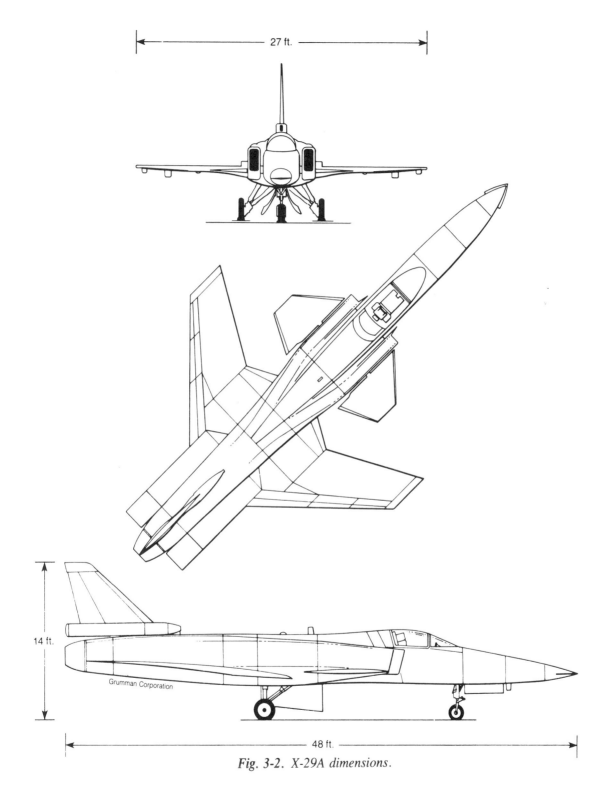

27 ft.

14 ft.

Grumman Corporation

48 ft.

*Fig. 3-2. X-29A dimensions.*

*Fig. 3-3. F-100D Super Sabre with 45-degree aft-swept flying surfaces.*

thrust class engine, its size and performance is nearly equal to a missioned fighter with a 30,000-pound thrust class engine.

The X-29A's FSW spans 27 feet 2 1/2 inches; its gross wing area is 188.84 square feet. The leading edge of the wing sweeps forward 33 degrees, 44 minutes; the trailing edge sweeps forward 45 degrees. The wing is of multispar construction using an electron beam welded titanium alloy front spar and titanium root ribs. The rest of the FSW (sans the wing covers) is of conventional aluminum alloy construction. It is of the cantilever low/mid-wing monoplane type with a NASA-developed and satisfactorily tested thin supercritical wing section. The thickness/chord ratio is 6.2 percent at the root and 4.9 percent at the tip; it has zero dihedral and wing incidence is 6 degrees at WS (wing station) 20 to plus 0.8 degrees at WS 163.22. It features full-span, dual-hinged, camber- (curve-) changing trailing edge flaperons or a combination flap and aileron system.

## Wing Covers

Aeroelastic-tailoring of the one-piece tip-to-tip advanced composite material wing covers inhibits structural divergence (twist). As aerodynamic forces build up on the forward-swept wing, the wing tends to twist upward at the leading edge, mostly toward the tip. The orientation of the composite carbon

fibers, however, limits the twist or structural divergence and forces the wing to return to its initial state (FIG. 3-7).

The use of composite material wing covers results in a very strong and lightweight wing. A total of 752 crisscrossed tapes were used to construct the wing covers, which are composed of 156 layers at their thickest points; a zero, 90, and plus-or-minus 45-degree angular layup is used. These laminated skins form the upper and lower sides of the wing torsion box (FIGS. 3-8, and 3-9).

## Thin Supercritical Wing Section

The Grumman X-29A is the first aircraft ever to fly with the NASA-developed thin supercritical wing section—one-third the thickness of previously built supercritical wings (FIG. 3-10). The very thin supercritical wing employed by the X-29 was made possible by the inherent strength of the aeroelastically-tailored design of the X-29's advanced composite material wing construction process.

Air flowing over a wing moves more rapidly across the upper surface than the lower surface—in the subsonic regime. As an aircraft approaches transonic speed (Mach 0.80 or 600 mph), the airflow over the upper surface forms shock waves on the wing that cause buffeting and increased drag. The profile (cross section) of a thin, medium, or thick supercritical wing, with its thicker leading edge and flatter upper surface, delays and softens shock waves. Buffeting is lessened and drag is reduced with a supercritical wing. Wind tunnel tests and computer analyses have shown the many advantages of this type of airfoil; however, there are no production aircraft that employ either a thin or a thick supercritical wing. The McDonnell Douglas AV-8B Harrier II uses a supercritical wing profile between thin and thick, while the Boeing AFTI (Advanced Fighter Technology Integration) F-111 MAW (Mission Adaptive Wing) test aircraft employs a thick supercritical wing that evolved from a design that was built in the 1970 decade for research, and that was successfully flight-tested on a modified LTV F-8A Crusader by NASA, the developer of this type of wing.

The use of computer models and analyses

*Fig. 3-4. X-29A with forward-swept wings and aft-swept canards and vertical tail.*

reduced wind tunnel tests by about 10 percent compared to other new aircraft. As mentioned earlier, a radio-controlled scale model built and flown in 1977 verified the computer codes. As the program progressed, a 1/8-scale wind tunnel model was tested subsonically, transonically, and supersonically at angles of attack as high as 90 degrees. Model force, moment, and pressure data were acquired from a 1/2-scale structural wing model that was installed in the 16-foot transonic dynamic tunnel at NASA Langley.

### Variable Camber Device

A two-segment discrete variable camber device is installed on the trailing edge of the X-29A's FSW (FIG. 3-11). While the X-29A's forward-swept thin

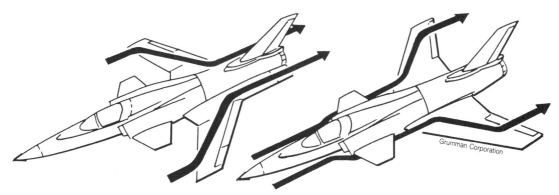

*Fig. 3-5. Reverse airflow: forward-swept wing versus aft-swept wing. On the FSW, ailerons remain unstalled at high AOA.*

supercritical wing provides excellent transonic performance and maneuverability, there is an excess of camber or curvature at the tailing edge of the wing for the aircraft to achieve efficient supersonic flight, thus its variable camber device.

This device varies the camber of the FSW in flight to the optimum configuration for all speeds and maneuvers, working too as a flaperon (combined flap and aileron) moving up and down to act as flaps and asymmetrically to act as ailerons. This allows the curvature of the wing to be altered in flight to create the best combination of lift and drag for takeoff, cruise, maneuvering, and landing. In simple terms, more of an aircraft's structure can now be trimmed to provide to optimum configuration for a certain speed and altitude.

### Close-Coupled Variable-Incidence Canard Foreplanes

The X-29A aircraft incorporates close-coupled variable-incidence canard foreplanes (FIGS. 3-12 and 3-13). These augment the X-29's lift, rather than causing drag as rear stabilator-type (combined stabilizer/elevator) tailplanes do. By being placed close to and in line with the wing, the canards provide basic pitch control (nose up/nose down), channel airflow over the inboard area of the wing to prevent root stall, and share the aerodynamic load with the wing. Their proximity to the wing led to the description *close-coupled canards*.

Each canard has a gross area that is 20 percent of the wing area or 94.42 square feet on either side of the fuselage; thus, 35.96 square feet each. Fully articulated, the leading edges of the canards move from 30 degrees up to 60 degrees down as the aerodynamic loads dictate on the aircraft. Canard construction is of conventional aluminum alloy buildup.

### Strake Flaps

Thirty-inch-long strake flaps on the trailing edge of the strakes augment the canards for pitch control. The strakes are the upward angled horizontal surfaces extending along both sides of the engine exhaust nozzle on the X-29A aircraft (FIG. 3-14). The strake flaps move through an arc of 30 degrees up and 30 degrees down (FIG. 3-15).

### Three-Surface Pitch Control

For its exceptional maneuverability, the X-29 uses a three-control-surface configuration for pitch control; the canards, flaperons, and strake flaps being driven in concert to minimize trim drag (FIG. 3-16). This, in turn, maximizes the aircraft's responsiveness at the onset of maneuvers by increasing pitch acceleration. The three flying surfaces, which in unison minimize the X-29's drag, are continuously driven: the canard for primary pitch control; the flaperons for roll control, high lift, and wing camber (curvature) changes; and the strake flaps to augment the canards at low speeds, which rotates the aircraft on takeoff or

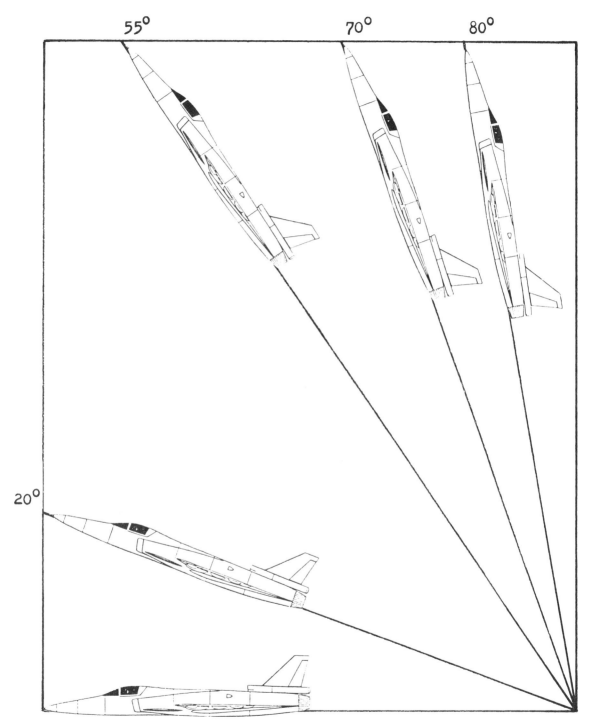

**Fig. 3-6.** *While X-29A-1 was only cleared to an AOA of 20 degrees, X-29A-2 may go up to an AOA of 90 degrees and still maneuver without any difficulty.*

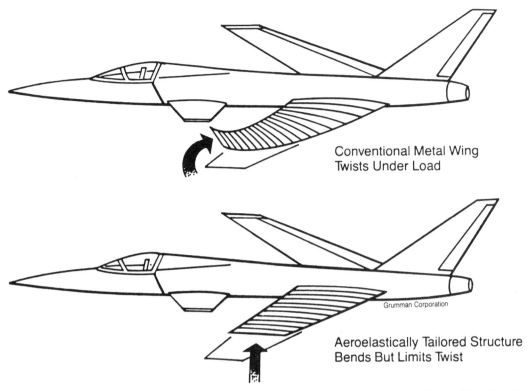

Conventional Metal Wing
Twists Under Load

Grumman Corporation

Aeroelastically Tailored Structure
Bends But Limits Twist

**Fig. 3-7.** *X-29A upper/lower wing covers are formed in one piece using aeroelastically-tailored composites.*

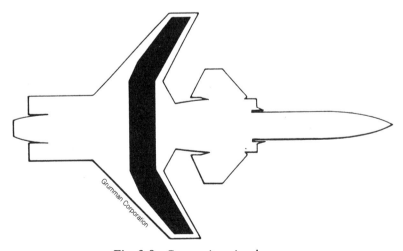

Grumman Corporation

**Fig. 3-8.** *Composite wing box.*

*Fig. 3-9. This photo of X-29A-1 under construction shows its one-piece composite wing box.*

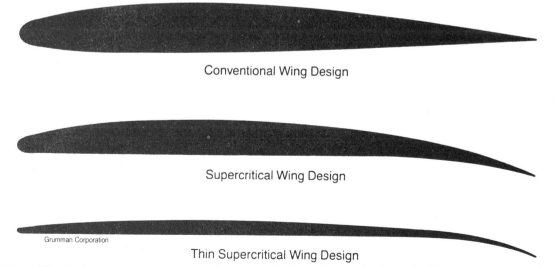

Conventional Wing Design

Supercritical Wing Design

Thin Supercritical Wing Design

*Fig. 3-10. Typical wing cross sections. Supercritical wing delays and softens shock waves on upper surface at transonic speeds.*

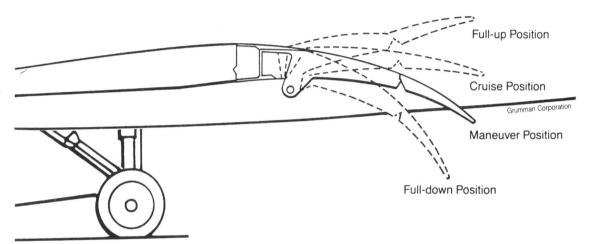

*Fig. 3-11.* Two-segment discrete variable camber device (side view) varies the camber (curvature) of the forward-swept wing in flight to the optimum configuration for all speeds and maneuvers.

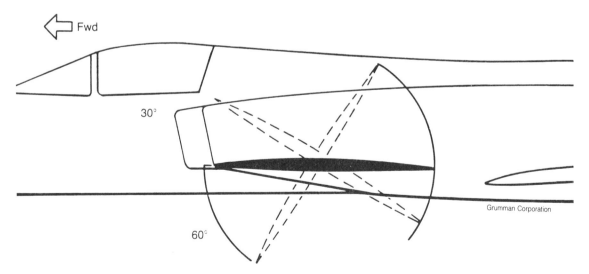

*Fig. 3-12.* Close-coupled variable incidence canards (side view) are X-29's primary pitch (nose-up, nose-down) control, which also share aerodynamic load with forward-swept wing.

**Fig. 3-13.** *Unusual view of X-29A-1 shows canard foreplanes.*

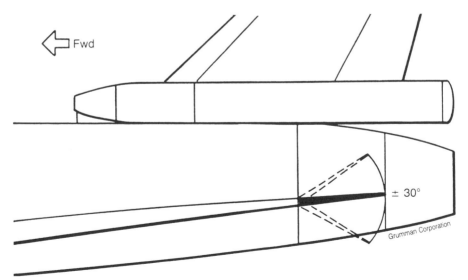

Fwd

± 30°

Grumman Corporation

**Fig. 3-14.** *Fuselage strake flaps are movable plus or minus 30 degrees (side view). They provide additional pitch (nose-up, nose-down) control, and work in concert with canards and variable camber flaperons.*

*Fig. 3-15. Strake flap is shown in this view of taxiing X-29A-1.*

pitches the aircraft down from a deep stall, or high AOA stall.

### Relaxed Static Stability

The X-29 incorporates relaxed static stability (RSS). Stability is the tendency of a conventionally configured aircraft (such as the F-15) to return to straight and level attitude flight after a movement of the controls. It is achieved at the cost of drag by balancing the lift loads on the wing with opposing downloads on the tailplane (FIG. 3-17). Achieving the highest degree ever, the X-29A aircraft are 35 percent unstable at subsonic speed. This inherent instability is called RSS or relaxed static stability. There are no stabilizing downloads on the X-29 because the canards share the lifting loads with the wing without benefit of rear stabilizers. Using a design with RSS reduces drag, but makes the aircraft difficult to control, because is must constantly be returned to straight and level attitude flight. But the X-29 has less drag, more maneuverability, and increased fuel efficiency with its designed-in relaxed static stability.

### Nose Strake

Grumman's X-29A aircraft employs a nose strake to eliminate unwanted side slip at high angles of attack, as the F-5A experienced; the F-5A's side slip would occur when its pitch-up angle (nose-up angle) was at about 40 degrees. The X-29's nose strakes are mounted on a horizontal plane in the center of its nose cones (FIG. 3-18).

### Systems

The two Grumman X-29A aircraft incorporate a number of advanced systems to accomplish their technology proof-of-concept parameters. One major system is the digital fly-by-wire (DFBW) flight control system (FCS).

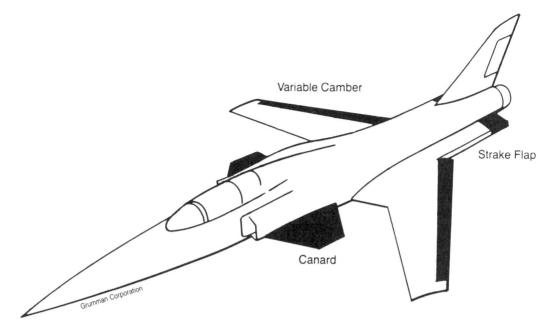

**Fig. 3-16.** *X-29 has three-surface pitch control; all surfaces work in unison to provide more maneuverability.*

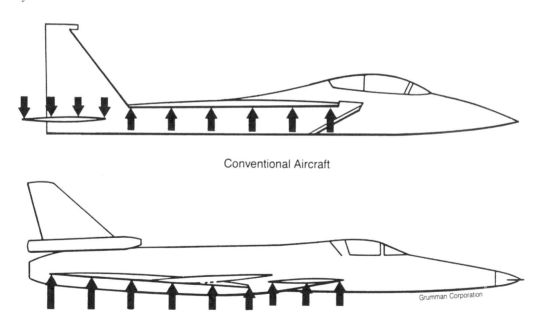

**Fig. 3-17.** *X-29A is designed with relaxed static stability to achieve less drag, more maneuverability, increased fuel efficiency. Arrows in upper illustration indicate drag-producing opposing downward forces on rear stabilizers to achieve stability. X-29 canards share lifting loads, reducing drag.*

*Fig. 3-18. X-29A nose strakes.*

## Digital Fly-By-Wire Flight Control System

A triply redundant, or triplex, digital flight control system of the fly-by-wire-type is used on the X-29A (FIG. 3-19). To control an aircraft designed with RSS, the DFCS must provide an artificial stability. On the X-29A this is achieved with a FBW-type digital FCS. Produced by Westinghouse, this system is a three-channel DFCS with an analog backup.

The X-29 aircraft have employed a number of software programs for various stages of their respective flight test phases; five are known, Block V through Block IX.

Fly-by-computer (or fly-by-wire) flight control systems enable the flying control surfaces of an aircraft to be operated by electronic command. Mechanical controls (such as steel braided and wound cables, pushrods, and bellcranks) on more conventional planes are replaced by computers, wires, buses, and sensors. To maneuver the X-29, the pilot moves the stick, which sends a command to the aircraft's flight control computer. The computer calculates the required control surface movements

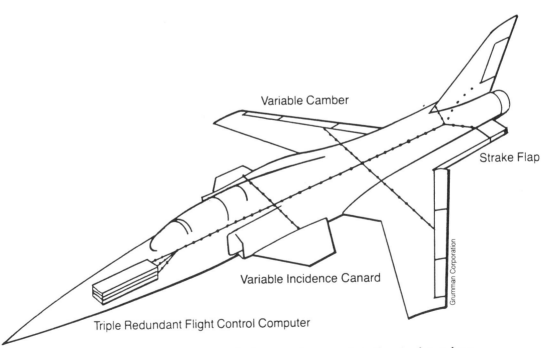

*Fig. 3-19. Digital fly-by-wire flight control system data flow is shown here.*

and sends a command to the actuator to move the control surfaces.

To maintain stability on the X-29, sensors assess flight conditions, including attitude, speed, and altitude, and feed data to the flight computer. It, in turn, continuously adjusts the control surfaces, transmitting up to 40 commands per second. The flight control computer coordinates the movements of all the control surfaces so that they work in unison.

As mentioned above, the DFCS on the X-29 is triply redundant, i.e., three control systems work in concert. Each system consists of a digital and an analog computer as well as their respective power supplies. If one digital system fails, the remaining two digital systems take over. If two digital computers fail, the flight control system switches to the analog mode. If one of the analog computers fails, the two remaining analog computers take over. The risk of failure in the X-29A's computerized flight control system is less than the risk of incurring a mechanical failure in a conventional system.

Using digital technology for aircraft flight control functions is relatively new. In a digital system, baseline data are programmed into the software. This makes a digital system easier to modify than its analog counterpart, which demands hardware modifications.

## Powerplant

The Grumman X-29A FSW technology demonstrator aircraft, like an ever-growing list of other reliable high-performance aircraft—such as the Lockheed F-117A Stealth fighter, McDonnell Douglas F/A-18 Hornet, and Rockwell/MBB's X-31A—are powered by the highly respected General Electric F404 fanjet engine. The X-29A employs the 16,000-pound thrust augmented (or afterburning) F404-GE-400 version (FIG. 3-20).

The outstanding turbojet characteristics of the F404 fanjet were demonstrated in its prototype version, the YJ101 (FIGS. 3-21, 3-22). The YJ101 turbojet engine in the Northrop YF-17 flight test program accumulated more than 700 flights and 1,200 flight hours with no stalls (compressor), no flight restrictions, and no afterburner blowouts throughout the flight envelope. In the F/A-18 Hornet (which was derived from the YF-17), the production F404 fanjet engine is even more impressive—and the F404 has proved to be well-suited to the X-29As.

The F404-GE-400 fanjet features 16,000 pounds thrust at a weight of 2,180 pounds dry for a 7.339-to-1 engine thrust-to-weight ratio. Its maximum diameter is 35 inches (2 feet, 11 inches); maximum length is 159 inches (13.25 feet). It is in the 25-to-1 pressure ratio class, and it has an airflow of 142 pounds per second.

General Electric

*Fig. 3-20. General Electric F404-GE-400 fanjet engine.*

*Fig. 3-21. Prototype F404, the YJ101.*

The F404-GE-400 fanjet engine is noted for its rapid throttle response—fast acceleration and deceleration, smooth and consistent afterburner light, and unrestricted throttle movements. It is of modular construction and has three fan stages and seven compressor stages. It is called the "fighter pilot's engine." The X-29 pilots, all of whom have flown fighters, are glad it powers their ride as well.

## Technologies Integration

Each of the technologies described in this chapter contributes to the X-29A FSW technology demonstrator program. They are integrated within the two aircraft to provide features appropriate to future military and commercial aircraft. Anticipated advantages include:

*Fig. 3-22. YF-17 prototypes were powered by two YJ101s; prototype F404.*

- *Improved agility,* providing unrestrained air combat maneuvering capability at high angles of attack.
- *Low-speed control,* providing positive aircraft positioning capability during landing approach and air combat maneuvers.
- *Transonic aerodynamic efficiency,* leading to smaller, lighter, and more efficient aircraft.
- *Low approach speed,* reducing landing distance requirements, which will open up more locations for aircraft deployment.
- *Reduced wing twist,* simplifying the wing design to cope with aerodynamic requirements for both high-speed cruise and transonic maneuvers of forward-swept wing aircraft.
- *Configuration versatility,* providing the aircraft designer with options for integrating future requirements such as 2-D (two-dimensional) exhaust nozzles and advanced cockpit designs.

Tests were conducted on the X-29A airplane itself and on a laboratory model housed in Grumman's Bethpage facility. The entire digital and analog flight control system underwent extensive testing. Simulators allowed pilots to experience realistic flight conditions. A hybrid simulation computer used a mathematical model of the X-29's flight characteristics to operate the laboratory's flight control system. Intensive testing was conducted using multiple failures, severe maneuvers, and flight outside the design envelope.

Another systems development tool was the TIFS (total in-flight simulator). Full X-29A flight controls were fitted in a separate cockpit extending from the nose of an Air Force C-131 aircraft. Using this simulator, pilots could experience hands-on control responses using the fly-by-wire flight control systems with varying software modifications.

In other ground tests, hydraulic pressures of the X-29's actuators and other components were monitored by the X-29 hydraulic test stand. Final acceptance ground tests were performed on the aircraft itself to evaluate the flight control, hydraulic, electrical, fuel, and environmental control systems.

While a pilot flies the X-29, flight data are transmitted to a ground station via a telemetry link. Using the ATS (automated telemetry system), constant communication and coordination are maintained between the aircraft and the ground. Temperatures in various sections of the plane, structural loads, wing pressures, bank angles, roll rates, angle of attack, and vibration are all reported to ground-based test engineers. Information is displayed on terminals while other computers feed data on graph paper, translating electronic transmissions into readable engineering data. Pilots and flight test engineers react to and address problems as they arise, and adjust the flight regime to achieve maximum performance and safety.

The flight test data is transmitted from NASA's ATS via satellite to Grumman's Calverton facility. The elapsed time between transmissions and computer display, California to New York, is about a quarter of a second.

## Configuration

The X-29A's configuration is roughly comparable to contemporary small fighter types such as the General Dynamics F-16 and Northrop F-5/F-20 series with a length of 48 feet, a span of 27 feet, and a height of 14 feet. Its maximum takeoff weight is 17,303 pounds, of which 3,978 pounds is JP-5 fuel; its empty weight is 13,326 pounds.

The X-29A aircraft is characterized by its relatively small forward-swept wing, a forward fuselage supporting a canard, an intermediate fuselage supporting the wing, and an aft fuselage which houses the engine and supports the single vertical tail, strakes, and strake flaps. The nose landing gear is housed within the forward fuselage section; the main landing gear is housed within the intermediate fuselage area.

The X-29A has two bladder-type fuel cells within the fuselage, a forward fuel tank and a fuel transfer tank, and an integral tank in each wing strake, giving a total capacity of 3,978 pounds.

Painted white for better visibility, the X-29A aircraft has a broad accent stripe of dark blue on its fuselage and wings outlined with a narrow red stripe. The red, white, and blue paint scheme emphasizes the forward-swept wings; X-29A-2 has an additional blue stripe outlined in red on its right wingtip (running fore to aft) and vertical fin top (running horizontally) to distinguish it from X-29A-1.

## Specifications

| | |
|---|---|
| Wingspan | 27 feet 2 1/2 inches |
| Wing Area | 188.84 square feet |
| Wing Chord (at root) | 9 feet 8 1/2 inches |
| Wing Chord (at tip) | 3 feet 11 inches |
| Wing Aspect Ratio | 4 |
| Canard Span | 13 feet 7 1/2 inches |
| Canard Area | 35.96 square feet |
| Length Overall, including nose probe | 53 feet 11 1/4 inches |
| Length of Fuselage | 48 feet 1 inch |
| Height Overall | 14 feet 3 1/2 inches |
| Vertical Tail Area (total) | 32.51 square feet |
| Wheel track | 7 feet 6 1/2 inches |
| Wheelbase | 17 feet 11 3/4 inches |

# 4

# Flight Testing X-29A
# Number One

FLIGHT TESTING of X-29A number one—by contract—began with four CEFs (contractor evaluation flights), all of which were to be flown by Grumman Chief Test Pilot and X-29A project pilot Charles A. (Chuck) Sewell. During the four CEFs the airplane was to be taken to a maximum speed of 0.60 Mach and a maximum altitude of 15,000 feet to test its basic airworthiness for its subsequent government Phase One flights. The latter would begin with flight number five, to be flown by Air Force and NASA pilots with continued Grumman pilot participation. With the one exception of Mother Nature, all entities were ready.

### Contractor Evaluation Flights

As the first contractor evaluation flight date approached, an intense low brought in a weather system of high winds and heavy rain. This unusual weather dumped 7/10ths of an inch of rain on Edwards on 10 December 1984 alone, making the dry lake bed wet and flight impossible; winds kicked up to 60 knots the next day. It was not safe to fly the premier X-29A until 14 December.

Sewell was ready. In fact, he had climbed into the X-29's cockpit about one hour and 45 minutes before takeoff.

At 9:35:30 A.M. (Pacific Time) Sewell released the brakes, advanced the throttle, and guided the world's first trans- and supersonic-capable forward-swept winged airplane into the blue skies above the Mojave Desert (FIGS. 4-1, 4-2). His liftoff of the red, white, and blue X-29A came at 9:35:40 A.M., and 156 knots, to begin what proved to be a highly successful maiden flight. Immediately after liftoff, the sleek airplane soared to an altitude of 15,000 feet in about three minutes. After leveling off, Sewell guided Grumman's first X airplane through a series of FCF (functional check flight) aerial maneuvers including pitch, roll, and yaw. Then he lowered altitude 5,000 feet, where he repeated all maneuvers. A maximum speed of 0.43 Mach (216 kias) was attained during the 66-minute test hop. The

*Fig. 4-1.* X-29A number one taking off for its first time on 14 December 1984.

*Fig. 4-2.* X-29A-1's first takeoff from another angle.

airplane was flown with its landing gear extended and its flaperons fully cambered throughout the flight (FIG. 4-3).

Several test landings were performed at an altitude of 8500 feet before the airplane was returned to the vicinity of the runway for the first of two scheduled approaches prior to actual landing (FIG. 4-4). Sewell brought the aircraft down to about 25 feet above the runway on the first pass, then accelerated and flew a wide right-hand racetrack pattern around the base before landing (FIG. 4-5). The X-29 appeared very steady in both approaches

Grumman Corporation

*Fig. 4-3. X-29A-1 flying at 15,000 feet and 216 knots with its landing gear down and locked, fixed camber on its flaps.*

*Fig. 4-4.* X-29A-1 during the first of two landing approaches, 25 feet above the runway.

and its landing was smooth. Sewell landed at 10:32 A.M., flying 12 minutes longer than planned, with 300 pounds more fuel than expected.

Grumman's fledgling had flown very well indeed but it had met moderate to heavy turbulence, which caused airspeed transients of plus/minus three to four knots, according to Sewell. He had radioed to the two chase T-38 pilots/observers to make sure that the condition was not being caused by the X-29's flight control system.

"The aircraft flew smoothly all the way up. I just wanted to make sure that it was the turbulence causing the buffeting and not the aircraft," Sewell said. "Looking out to either side, the T-38s were

*Fig. 4-5.* X-29A-1's first landing.

gyrating more in the turbulence. My flight control system seemed to be taking out the perturbations. I couldn't see my wing moving and I didn't notice the canard moving much.''

Grumman test officials were not surprised by the X-29's reactions in the turbulence. ''The flight control system tries to dampen out disturbances,'' Grumman's Glenn Spacht said. ''It did what we had hoped.''

Sewell had nothing but praise for the ''Grummanites'' on the X-29A team. ''They're outstanding,'' he said after his familiarization flight. ''There is no better team to work with in the world.''

The second CEF was scheduled for 18 December, but a very rare snowfall covered Edwards and no more X-29 flights occurred in 1984. It took more than a month for Edwards to dry out.

Sewell conducted the second and third CEFs on 4 and 22 February 1985, respectively. During these two HQE (handling qualities evaluation) flights, the aircraft's JFS (jet fuel starter), EPU (emergency power unit), and landing gear were tested thoroughly; a SFO (simulated flame-out) on approach was made. Both flights were successful, but near the end of flight number three, Sewell did a maneuver that wasn't part of the flight plan—a roll. Because of this action, the Air Force barred (not grounded per se) him from conducting the fourth and final CEF. Instead, Grumman X-29A co-project pilot Kurt C.

Shroeder flew the fourth CEF on 1 March 1985, a pilot familiarization flight with AOA (angle of attack) instrument calibration.

The USAF and NASA accepted X-29A-1 after Grumman's fourth CEF—on 12 March 1985, USAF; 22 March 1985, NASA. It was now time to begin government Phase One.

### Government Phase One

With Grumman's continued participation, flights five through 104 were government Phase One flights. This first phase, which lasted one year and eight months, was conducted to check all of the aircraft's systems in action (FIG. 4-6).

To begin Phase One, flights five through seven were flown by the three assigned X-29A government pilots: Steve Ishmael, NASA X-29A project pilot; Lt. Col. Ted Wierzbanowski, AFFTC X-29A program manager and test pilot; and Rogers Smith, NASA X-29A co-project pilot, respectively. Government and Grumman pilots flew the airplane on a rotational basis. Each pilot, to a man, had high praise for the FSW technology demonstrator and could not wait for his turn to come up again.

Before Phase One ended, two more government pilots flew X-29A-1: AFFTC X-29A program manager and test pilot Lt. Col. (then Maj.) Harry C. Walker III, who replaced Wierzbanowski; and U.S. Navy Lt. Cdr. Ray Craig, a guest pilot who flew two

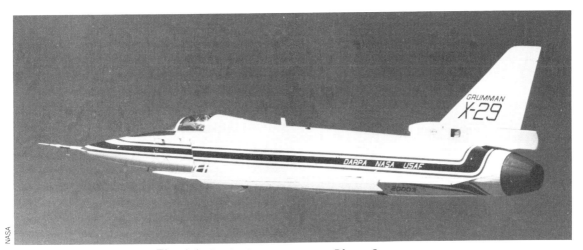

*Fig. 4-6. Beginning government Phase One.*

FQE (flying qualities evaluation) flights (numbers 103 and 104) to end Phase One. Craig was the only Navy pilot to fly the airplane.

The X-29's performance envelope was very carefully expanded during the initial phase—.6 Mach to .7M, .7M to .8M, .8M to .9M, then to .94 Mach—flights five through 25. The aircraft's stability and control were exceptional in the low- to high-subsonic regime and in the low-transonic speed range, at all altitudes flown up to 41,113 feet. It became time to challenge the higher end of the transonic speed range—to actually go supersonic or 1.0 Mach in a forward-swept wing aircraft for the first time. NASA's Steve Ishmael got the nod to fly this historic aviation event.

It was 13 December 1985, during flight number 26 (Ishmael's sixth), that a straight and level attitude speed of 1.03 Mach at 40,000 feet was attained by X-29A-1. The aircraft's first supersonic flight was accomplished without problem; in fact, the transition from subsonic to supersonic speed was so smooth that the occurrence had to be verified by instrumentation. Of course, this historic occasion was celebrated by all entities. Norris Krone and Glenn Spacht were particularly overjoyed with the event, because they had finally been rewarded for their respective efforts.

Up until 20 December the airplane had been flown one or two times a day, but this day marked the first time it had been flown three times in one day—3.6 total hours, by three different pilots. June 12, 1986, marked the first time it was flown four times in one day—3.4 total hours, three pilots, one going up twice. The X-29's turnaround time was becoming somewhat like that of a missionized fighter.

Between flights number 26 and 104, X-29A-1 flew 52 supersonic flights and registered some impressive accomplishments, especially for an X airplane. Highlights are as follows: It attained a maximum Mach number of 1.46 at 50,200 feet, nearly 1,000 mph; it flew at 1.10M at 10,000 feet, subjecting the airframe to a maximum dynamic pressure load (termed max q) of 1,300 pounds per square foot; it sustained a 5.7G turn at .7M at 10,000 feet (a 5.7G turn means the X-29's wings bear 5.7

times their normal, level flight loads); it flew under control up to an AOA of 22 degrees; and it exceeded its maneuver design point performance goal by achieving a lift-to-drag ratio of 6.7 at .9M at 30,000 feet (this excess performance translates to a reduced turning radius).

More importantly, the X-29A FSW technology demonstrator validated the concept of aeroelastically-tailored, thin supercritical, advanced composite material wing construction and showed that the divergence boundary (conditions beyond which flight loads could force the wings to bend to the breaking point) lay at least 15 percent beyond the design envelope.

A little over two years after its first flight, government Phase One ended on 23 December 1986. The aircraft was subsequently placed in a NASA hangar for updating in preparation for its more vigorous second phase.

**Government Phase Two**

Government Phase Two flights of X-29A-1 did not begin until it got a number of scheduled modifications. These alterations kept the X-29 in the hangar and on the ground for some six months.

Government Phase One culminated after 100 flights; Government Phase Two required another 138 flights, which lasted one year and six months—from 19 June 1987 to 8 December 1988.

Grumman, NASA, and USAF technicians readied X-29A-1 for Phase Two while it was in its hangar. In part, a new and specially calibrated F404-GE-400 fanjet engine was installed, as was an updated Block VII DFCS software package for more agressive maneuvers. Moreover, its instrumentation was updated. The aircraft was now free to resume flight testing.

Grumman's Ron Feddersen explained why the specially calibrated F404 engine was required for Phase Two:

"In level, steady-state flight, the airplane's equilibrium is maintained by equal amounts of thrust and drag. No way has yet been found to measure either one accurately in flight, so the standard method is to calculate engine thrust under given conditions and, from it, the drag.

"The problem is that production powerplants show differences, engine to engine. Their thrust can thus only be roughly determined from averaged information obtained from the manufacturer based on experience and ground tests.

"As the X-29 contractor, Grumman's initial design concern was the generalized shapes of the curves of lift and drag, so we were able to use an uncalibrated engine. But NASA and USAF have different goals, and one of them is to measure very precisely the small change in performance that come about with minor changes in airplane configuration.

"Consequently, a complete General Electric F404-GE-400 fanjet engine together with its associated instrumentation was submitted to testing in a wind tunnel at NASA's Lewis Research Center and calibrated so that thrust, fuel flow, air flow, temperatures, and other parameters were correlated. That meticulous program resulted in an engine with known quantities. . .and known variations of those quantities. In the X-29A, this engine will enable NASA to determine performance and performance increments with great accuracy."

Government Phase Two flight testing began officially on 19 June 1987 (flight number 105) with NASA's Steve Ishmael. It was a FCF, coupled with the aircraft's updated Block VII DFCS software release, and AOA and airspeed calibrations. The 50-minute test hop was a very smooth flight to begin Phase Two (FIG. 4-7).

During Phase One, X-29A-1 had devoted itself to what is known in flight test circles as "expanding the flight envelope," a process that involved flying the airplane at controlled conditions over a wide range of speeds and altitudes. This particular envelope can be plotted as a curve of aerodynamic parameters that define how slow, how fast, and how high the aircraft can go in level, steady-state flight. Other envelopes can be developed for other conditions of flight, such as steady turns and so forth.

The lessons learned have been many. The 100 flights logged in Phase One proved that a highly unstable aircraft—and therefore a very maneuverable, agile one—can be flown safely and reliably. The X-29 demonstrated that it can maneuver better at transonic speeds (.8M to 1.2M) than its high-powered missionized fighter contemporaries with their more conventional aft-swept wings. At equivalent values of drag, the FSW produced a 15 percent increase in lift, a higher sustained G-load in turns, and a smaller turn radius. These results are quite remarkable, considering that they were achieved despite the aircraft being operated under constraints.

During the second phase of its flight research program, which took it to a maximum Mach number of 1.48 and an altitude of 50,707 feet, X-29A-1 was flown, in a number of fighter-like maneuvers, into new regions of performance with potential payoffs—DARPA's primary concern (FIG. 4-8).

A most unusual feature demonstrated by X-29A-1 had nothing to do with its forward-swept wing planform or its ability to fly like a fighter-type aircraft: It showed from the start that it was far more reliable than any previous X-type air vehicle. The plane was flown four times in a single day on a number of occasions. It was also flown seven times in one week, 17 times in one month. In fact, there were occasions when the pacing element of the test program was the time required to process and review the computerized data.

During Phase Two, Steve Ishmael and Rogers Smith stayed on as the NASA pilots. Major Alan D. (Al) Hoover flew flights number 159 and 161 on 13 and 22 January 1988 to replace Lt. Col. Walker as AFFTC X-29A program manager and test pilot. And Grumman's Rod Womer flew flight number 148 on 4 December 1987 to replace Kurt Schroeder.

During its two-phase, four-year flight test program, X-29A-1 flew a record number of flights for an X-type aircraft. The record was established on 8 June 1988, when it flew its 200th test hop (during which it simulated an inflight refueling with a KC-135), exceeding the old mark of 199 flights set by a North American X-15 on 24 October 1968; NASA's Rogers Smith flew flight 200 as well as X-29A-1's last (FIG. 4-9).

Government Phase Two ended on 8 December 1988 with flight number 242. The airplane was flown four times on that date by four different pilots—two assigned and two guest pilots. Total

*Fig. 4-7. X-29A-1's 105th flight, beginning Phase Two.*

flight time for the airplane was 178.6 hours, for an average of 1.35 hours per flight.

Following its last flight, X-29A-1 was placed in flyable storage, a condition in which all main systems are retained in the aircraft and it could be returned to flight status within a specific period of time. It is being maintained inside one of NASA's hangers. There are no current plans to modify the airplane for any follow-on flight test program.

## Summary

"We have proven that the design is variable," said NASA's current X-29A project manager, Gary Trippensee (FIG. 4-10). "Our next step is to look at low-speed, high angle-of-attack characteristics of a forward-swept wing aircraft using X-29A number two."

Trippensee became the third NASA X-29A project manager in July of 1986, replacing Walter J.

*Fig. 4-8. X-29A-1 in flight during first supersonic test flight.*

*Fig. 4-9. X-29A-1's 200th test hop, simulating inflight refueling.*

*Fig. 4-10. NASA X-29 program manager Gary Trippensee.*

(Wally) Sefic, who was preceded by Terry Putnam.

Trippensee said the X-29 has had no problems structurally. "No cracks, no wrinkles, and no evidence of any structural problems have ever been found. One minor, extremely small delamination of the wing skin of the number one X-29A was found, but this was subsequently determined to be a manufacturing defect."

In light of X-29A-2, Trippensee said, "There are 50 to 70 flights planned for X-29A number two, assuming there is satisfactory funding to complete the planned program." He concluded, "The number two X-29 aircraft simulation shows the maximum trim angle-of-attack to be approximately 70 degrees with full aft stick. This is the maximum AOA to be evaluated in flight."

# 5

# Flight Testing X-29A
# Number Two

FLIGHT TESTING of X-29A number two was to begin in the spring of 1987. However, the required funding for its follow-on flight test activities was slow to materialize. Therefore, X-29A-2 was forced to stay in extended storage at Grumman's Calverton facility for five years after it had been used in the type's formal rollout ceremony in 1984—an extraordinary length of time for a completed X airplane especially and an unprecedented length of time for any airplane. Nevertheless, X-29A number two survived its period of confinement and is now plying the skies over Edwards, following in the footsteps of its highly successful sister ship.

Earlier, in May of 1985, Grumman proposed the use of X-29A-2 for a high alpha (high angle of attack) flight test program. The idea was to increase the rate of data collection, according to Grumman. "We suggest that the second ship be tested at high angles of attack while the first one continues with high-speed tests," Glenn Spacht said. "That way, we can gather data more quickly than if we wait to test the first ship for high angle of attack performance."

You may recall that X-29A-1 was limited to about 20 degrees angle of attack. The idea here was to push X-29A-2 50 degrees above that, to 70 degrees AOA—or more, if justified.

The estimated cost to prepare X-29A-2 over an 11-month period was $6.2 million in May of 1985; the amount eventually decreased. Preparation at Calverton was to include completion of the aircraft's instrumentation to allow automatic telemetry of flight data to ground stations, installation of an anti-spin parachute to recover the aircraft from possible spins due to stall (loss of lift) during high AOA maneuvers and, of course, updated DFCS software programs.

The DARPA, USAF, and NASA agreed on the plan to conduct high AOA tests with X-29A-2 in December of 1985. The Air Force Flight Dynamics Laboratory (AFFDL) at Wright-Patterson AFB authorized Grumman to design airframe and systems modifications for the high alpha flight test program under a $4.6 million contract—$1.6 million less than Grumman's original request—and the airplane was to be modified at Bethpage instead of Calverton. At this time, the high alpha flight test phase was scheduled to start in the spring of 1987 at NASA's Ames-Dryden FRF, where its sister ship was still flying. Additionally, only about 35 flights to a maximum AOA of 40 degrees were planned, with excursions up to 70 degrees AOA.

A two-year delay ensued, during which renegotiations modified the high alpha flight test program to include some 50 to 70 flights to a 70 degree AOA with excursions up to 90 degrees. According to Grumman, it should be noted, the X-29A airplane is designed for full controllability over the complete plus-to-minus 90 degree angle of attack range.

Four veteran X-29A-1 pilots are assigned to fly X-29A-2. Grumman's pilot is Rod Womer, AFFTC X-29A project manager/test pilot is Major Al Hoover (now Dana Puritoy), NASA X-29A project pilot is Steve Ishmael, and NASA X-29A co-project pilot is Rogers Smith. Just as these pilots flew X-29A-1, they will fly X-29A-2 on a rotational basis. No other pilots have been announced at this writing (February 1990).

After modifications, X-29A-2 took its cruise to California via the Panama Canal (FIG. 5-1). The airplane, complete with its protective covering, traveled by government ship to Port Hueneme, California, and then trucked to Edwards on 7 November 1988 (FIG. 5-2). It was then put in the very same hangar occupied by the number one X-29A, where it was prepared for its high alpha flight test program (FIG. 5-3). At the time, X-29A-1 still had 17 flights to perform. It would take a little over six months to prepare X-29A-2 for flight testing.

NASA's Rogers Smith performed X-29A-2's high-speed taxi test on 20 May 1989, which culminated with the deployment and jettison of the anti-

*Fig. 5-1. X-29A-2 was wrapped in protective covering for its ocean voyage to California.*

*Fig. 5-2. X-29A-2 was trucked overland to Edwards from Port Hueneme, California.*

*Fig. 5-3. X-29A-2 (foreground) in NASA hangar with X-29A-1.*

spin parachute. To begin, Smith accelerated the vehicle to a speed of 120 knots in military power. He throttled back slightly at this speed and applied about 1 to 1 1/2 inches of aft stick. The airplane rotated to a nose-up (pitch) attitude of about 10 degrees at this time. The nose gear wheel came off the runway and the main gear struts extended but the main gear wheels did not lift from the runway; maximum speed before deceleration was about 140 knots. As it slowed to about 70 knots, Smith advanced the throttle slightly. Then, at about 90 knots, Smith deployed the chute. A maximum speed of some 100 knots occurred before chute-enticed deceleration came about. The deployment caused a slight nose-up pitch of about two degrees; a slight nose-left yaw of some two to three degrees occurred as well, possibly due to a five-knot crosswind. Smith jettisoned the chute at about 72 knots without any noticeable transients. He noted that the aircraft's pitch response during the high-speed taxi was very impressive at its gross weight of 16,000-plus pounds (nearly maximum) and that there was nothing abnormal.

### First Flight

NASA's Steve Ishmael performed the premier flight of X-29A-2 on 23 May 1989 (FIGS. 5-4 THROUGH 5-6). This was a 54-minute test hop; maximum speed and altitude were 0.60 Mach at 28,500 feet on this FCF (functional check flight). Ishmael observed that it flew fine, with takeoff similar to the number one aircraft. He noted that there was an approximate there was an approximate four-degree right wing down transient when downmoding from ND (normal digital) to AR (analog reversion) modes on the flight control system, and during the steady heading sideslips performed at 165 knots and 10,000 feet, there was a strong proverse roll when 10 degrees of bank were exceeded. And, unlike X-29A-1, the fuel transfer from the strake tanks was complete; X-29A-1 always carried residual fuel that would not empty.

The second flight, another FCF, was flown by Maj. Al Hoover on 13 June. The aircraft was taken to 0.95M at 23,400 feet, but while it was at its maximum altitude of 30,000 feet, Hoover investigated 10, 15 and 18 degrees AOA. He observed that X-29A-2 has much better pitch authority than did X-29A-1 at low airspeed (0.30M), and that takeoff was smooth without transients—unlike X-29A-1, which had a tendency to jump off the runway.

### Spin Chute Testing

Steve Ishmael flew flight number three on the same day, specifically to deploy and jettison the spin chute at high speed (FIGS. 5-7, 5-8). The chute was deployed at 180 knots and 25,000 feet, jettisoned at 150 knots and 17,000 feet. Ishmael reported the aircraft handled well under chute loads, but was sluggish in pitch maneuvers. There was a noticeable fore-and-aft motion with the chute deployed and the chute caused more drag than predicted in the X-29 flight simulator. The aircraft attitude stabilized five

*Fig. 5-4. X-29A-2's first takeoff.*

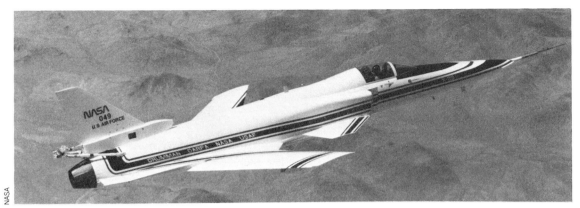

*Fig. 5-5. X-29A-2's premier flight.*

*Fig. 5-6. X-29A-2's first landing.*

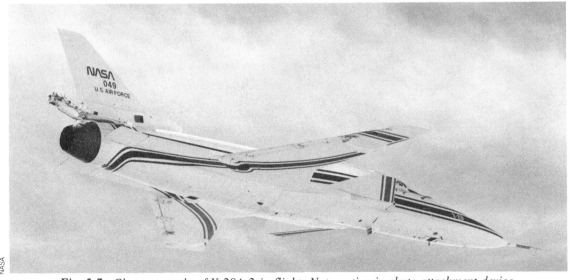

*Fig. 5-7. Close-up study of X-29A-2 in flight. Note anti-spin chute attachment device.*

to 10 degrees more nose-low than the simulator had predicted, and there was a noticeable pitch-down motion at chute separation. Due to the large drag effect, Ishmael noted that landing with the chute attached is not practical. He did, however, have praise for the design of a highly efficient and reliable system for recovering of aircraft from a low energy (low-speed) state departure (stall).

While the purpose of flight number three was the high-speed qualification of the aircraft's anti-spin chute, flight number four was for its low-speed qualification. Flown by Maj. Hoover on 23 June, the chute was deployed at 120 knots and 25,000 feet, jettisoned at 140 knots and 17,000 feet. Hoover observed that aircraft attitude did not change much during deployment of the chute, and that the large longitudinal deceleration experienced during the high-speed deployment on the previous flight was not apparent. Aircraft response was very smooth with the chute attached; a fairly constant attitude was observed during chute jettison. Hoover suggested that future chute jettisons should be performed at engine flight idle power.

Respectively, flights five, six, seven and eight were flown by Rogers Smith, Rod Womer, Steve Ishmael, and Al Hoover. These consisted mostly of flight controls clearance, airspeed calibration, functional checks, airdata calibration, SFO practice, radar calibration, and high alpha clearance to 20 degrees AOA.

Smith and Womer flew flights nine and ten respectively, both on 8 November 1989. Both flights featured maximum angles of attack to 22.5 degrees, the highest yet. At 15 and 16 degrees AOA the aircraft experienced vibrations, which subsided at 20-plus degrees AOA. At an AOA of 22.5 degrees, however, aircraft performance was predictable, solid, and controllable.

Flights 11 and 12, on 28 November and 19 December respectively, rounded out the year 1989. Then, in January 1990, when X-29A-2 flight testing resumed, some extraordinary things began to happen.

According to NASA X-29A Project Manager Gary Trippensee, all of the flight test parties involved have realized a number of exciting flight

*Fig. 5-8. X-29A-2's third flight tested high-speed (180 knots) spin chute deployment.*

results with the number two X-29A. It was during January 1990 that all entities started scrambling to understand why X-29A-2 showed flight test results at high AOA much better than predicted. It was flown six times in January up to a maximum AOA of 40 degrees—and flew extremely well, especially above 22 degrees AOA. The Air Force, NASA, and Grumman (DARPA is no longer associated with the program) are trying to get a clearly defined understanding of the aero mechanisms associated with these unpredicted high-alpha improvements. As of 15 February 1990, X-29A-2 has reached 50 degrees AOA and is continuing to impress those associated with the program. Maj. Hoover called the airplane a "tiger," and said, "We have it by the tail."

### Summary

As discussed earlier in text, the number two X-29A will fly 50 to 70 flights up to a maximum angle of attack of 70 degrees before its currently planned flight test program is concluded. An extended test program to even higher AOA has been rumored.

It now appears that X-29A-1 will go to the NASM (National Air and Space Museum) at Washington, DC in the near future—a fitting end to a history-making airplane. What becomes of X-29A-2, if you will pardon the pun, is still up in the air, but most likely it will be retired to the AFM (Air Force Museum) at Dayton, Ohio.

While the number one X-29A remains in a hangar, the number two X-29A continues to perform extremely well while its high angle-of-attack flight test envelope is carefully expanded. This preplanned slow expansion process will continue until its maximum AOA and associated performance levels are realized (FIGS. 5-9 and 5-10).

NASA

*Fig. 5-9*. *X-29A-2 in a bank.*

**Fig. 5-10.** *Nice in-flight shot of X-29A-2 with chase T-38A.*

Grumman is famed for its production of great naval fighter types—ferocious felines such as its Hellcat, Bearcat, Tomcat, and others. But pay attention to the X-29A, Grumman's ''Straycat,'' as it continues to strut its stuff. This Grumman ''tiger'' could sire the shape of wings to come.

*The first X-29A nears completion.*

*First test installation of a GE F404 engine in the X-29A.*

*The instrument panel of the original X-29A. Note that Mach meter pegs at 1.5 Mach.*

U.S. Air Force

*The first X-29A lifts off, rapidly retracting its landing gear.*

NASA

*The original X-29A during its record-setting 200th flight.*

*The first X-29A banks over Edwards.*

*Excellent view of the first X-29A in flight.*

*The 200th flight of X-29A-1 was a record-setter for X planes.*

X-29A-1 prepares to land. Note the landing gear detail.

Details of X-29A-1 underside and canopy.

*An advanced version of the X-29 is depicted.*

*X-29A-1 goes over-the-top in a loop.*

*First flight of X-29A-2.*

# 6

# X-29A Pilots and Their Comments

<hr>

WHAT WAS it like to fly the X-29A aircraft, a forward-swept-wing X-plane with a number of other advanced technology features in particular? I collected a number of pilot comments, which are as follows:

### Charles Sewell

Charles A. (Chuck) Sewell, Grumman's ex-Chief Test Pilot and X-29A project pilot (FIG. 6-1), said that the X-29 was "... easy to fly, conventional from the pilot's point of view." Sewell made the first contractor evaluation flight after which he said: "For any plane—let alone an X-plane—to return after its first flight and not have any discrepancies, that's just super. Especially when it is eight steps forward in the state of the art. As far as I'm concerned, we can pump more fuel in the X-29 and I'd fly it again today." Sewell flew four more times in X-29A-1 before returning to Grumman for other duties related to his Chief Test Pilot status there. Unfortunately, two months after his return to Grumman, he was killed in the crash of a WWII-vintage torpedo bomber he was ferrying to Florida for a friend. It was a sad end to the career of an extraordinary pilot who logged more than 10,000 flying hours in 140 different types of aircraft, including the X-29.

### Kurt Schroeder

Kurt C. Schroeder, who replaced Chuck Sewell and became Grumman's Chief Test Pilot (FIG. 6-2), flew X-29A-1 23 times before he was replaced by Grumman's current X-29 project pilot, Rod Womer (FIG. 6-3). Schroeder said: "It flies like a small airplane. It's sensitive . . . but it feels like a much larger and more stable aircraft. With its high engine thrust-to-weight ratio and the responsiveness, it's similar to modern-day fighters. But it gets more performance out of a smaller wing than they do."

Schroeder added: "One of the fallouts of the high degree of its 35 percent instability is the X-29's excellent agility. To move quickly from one flight path to another, all you do is bump the controls a little to get the airplane moving, and then they

*Fig. 6-1. Charles A. (Chuck) Sewell.*

*Fig. 6-3. Rod Womer.*

*Fig. 6-2. Kurt C. Shroeder.*

immediately begin to apply corrective action to avoid overshooting—and that's with the conservative control laws that were used on the first X-29. With the second X-29, we are going to be much more agressive, because the engineers are changing the control laws to allow that. We're installing a spin chute, so if the airplane should inadvertently depart from controlled flight, we'd have a way to recover it.''

### Stephen Ishmael

Stephen D. (Steve) Ishmael, who flew X-29A-1 63 times and now flies X-29A-2 (FIG. 6-4), said of his experience with number one: ''It has very pleasant ride qualities, which is surprising. Some of today's fighters with the same characteristics are a nightmare

Fig. 6-4. Stephen D. (Steve) Ishmael.

the FSW has other advantages as well, you don't pay a penalty for going that route to gain, for example, exceptional lateral control. It feels like such a solid airplane when you taxi it. I fly the F-16 a lot, and it bounces around on taxi. But the X-29 taxis like it weighed 40,000 pounds.''

### Rogers Smith

Rogers E. Smith, who flew X-29A-1 56 times and now flies X-29A-2 (FIG. 6-5), began his comments at the other end of flight: ''In the landing pattern, handling qualities are excellent. It flies very precisely, very smoothly. You can land it instinctively.

Smith added: ''The engine-airplane combination is a good one. It's a very good engine, very

Fig. 6-5. Rogers E. Smith.

nightmare to fly on a low-level, high-speed penetration mission. But the X-29 has a real smooth ride, and we're going to investigate to see why. The handling qualities are the same at Mach 1.4 and 40,000 feet as they are at 250 knots and 5,000 feet. In fact, they're the same for most of the flight envelope. Toward the high-speed end, the airplane seemed a little sluggish longitudinally (side-to-side) and it didn't roll like a fighter. The forward-swept wing gives you better lateral (end-to-end) control for a longer time and to a higher angle of attack. So if responsive, very forgiving. The •X-29 has good climb in military power. If you go into afterburner, it really moves out. I think it has good fighter performance capabilities.''

Smith concluded: ''Another interesting aspect is that the three sets of control surfaces (canards, flaperons, and strakes) are constantly moving as you maneuver the airplane. But it's all very smooth and the integration of those three controls is transparent (unnoticed) to the pilot. If the airplane gets hit by a gust, the surfaces move rapidly to suppress the pitch and roll. The flight control system has proven very fault-free . . . no glitches. Its behavior has been impressive.''

### Theodore Wierzbanowski

Col. Theodore J. (Ted) Wierzbanowski (FIG. 6-6), ex-AFFTC C-29A Program Manager and Test Pilot, the first Air Force pilot to fly X-29A-1 (10 flights) before he was replaced by Lt. Col. Harry C. Walker III, stated succinctly: ''It's an airplane, and it flies like an airplane.''

### Harry Walker

Lt. Col. Walker, ex-AFFTC X-29A Program Manager and Test Pilot, who was replaced by Maj. Alan D. (Al) Hoover and flew X-29A-1 33 times, answered some specific questions:

**Q.** What is the X-29A's best climb rate?

**A.** ''We never specifically measured or tried to optimize the X-29A for climb performance and thus I cannot give a specific number that will hold for all conditions. We did measure the specific excess power of the airplane, and as we reported in our final performance report (X-29A-1), the X-29 could achieve a climb rate of 530 feet per second at 10,000 feet pressure altitude. This translates to an instantaneous rate of climb of 31,800 feet per minute. This number, however, is of little practical use in comparing aircraft. A better way to compare aircraft is with specific excess power for missionized aircraft (those that are operational such as the F-15 and F-16) or with drag polar shape and magnitude for research aircraft. In our case, we show an increase in performance measured as a decrease in induced drag

*Fig. 6-6. Lt. Col. Theodore J. (Ted) Wierzbanowski, known as W-plus-12.*

over the F-16 on the order of 20 to 45 percent depending on the flight condition. This measure too must be viewed in context, as the X-29 is a small demonstrator airplane compared to a missionized fighter. It does, however, point to the type and approximate levels of performance gains that can be realized with the type of X-29 technologies. Please remember, these numbers are for the X-29 as a total air vehicle, not just the forward-swept wing.''

**Q.** What is the X-29A's best roll rate?

**A.** ''The roll rate of the X-29 is a difficult number to pin down at a set value. It is a function of altitude and Mach number as well as which flight control configuration is in the aircraft. Roll rate in the X-29 was constrained by the flight control system (software program), as it is in many newer digital-type flight control systems, to prevent yaw divergence due to rolling moment. The X-29 was the first aircraft to fly with 35 percent static instability. Due to this high level of instability, the roll rate of the airplane was initially constrained to about 120 degrees per second. Later, the roll rate was increased to approximately 220 degrees per second as we gained more knowledge of the flight control characteristics of the vehicle. The increase in roll rate was accomplished by simply changing the gains in the flight control system and allowing the first X-29A airplane to get closer to its aerodynamic limits. The number two X-29A is currently involved in an agility study to measure the goodness of various rates of maneuver, and roll rate is one of these measurands.''

**Q.** According to its flight log, X-29A-1 made a number of WUTs or wind-up-turns. What is a wind-up-turn?

**A.** ''A WUT or wind-up-turn is a turn that slowly increases the parameter of interest as other parameters are held constant. Most of the time in the X-29 program (air vehicle number one), we flew constant Mach number and slowly increased the G or the angle of attack with a constant power setting. This resulted in a turn that was like a corkscrew as we increased to our limit for the flight at hand. With this maneuver we could then measure the change in G or the AOA as a function of thrust required and determine the performance of the airplane. We also used this maneuver to measure the loads of the vehicle and determine the structural integrity of the X-29.''

**Q.** The acronym MCC appears throughout X-29A-1's flight log. What does it mean?

**A.** ''The acronym MCC stands for Manual Camber Control. The X-29's flap tab system on the trailing edge of the wing automatically varied the camber (curvature) of the wing in flight to reduce drag. We could fix this system to set the flaps at a predetermined value. We could then fly at specific points in the envelope to help us pinpoint specific contributions of the aircraft's various technologies.''

**Q.** What was the highest Mach number attained during your tenure with X-29A number one?

**A.** ''We took X-29A number one to a Mach number (Mn) of 1.46 on its 100th flight. The airplane was designed to fly at a Mn of 1.2 and we only went to 1.46Mn to demonstrate structural integrity of the vehicle. The biggest limitation of its

$V_{max}$ (maximum speed) is its fixed-geometry engine air inlet, which was not designed for high Mach number flight.'' [*X-29A-1 flew to Mn of 1.48 on its 147th flight.*]

**Q.** How does the X-29 compare with some of the other missionized fighter types you have flown?

**A.** ''A very interesting and difficult question. The X-29 was a joy to fly because it was the only X airplane out there. Its handling qualities during envelope expansion were acceptable, but not the quality that I would want in a modern-day fighter. They did get better and are still being refined. The X-29's performance in the transonic speed range was impressive. For a small aircraft with a relatively small engine, it did very well. There are other aircraft that are faster, climb better, go farther, etc. But as a research aircraft to measure the state of the art in design technology, the X-29 did its job superbly.''

**Q.** Anything else you'd like to tell us about the aircraft?

**A.** ''The 35 percent instability was such an unknown that Grumman built a very conservative basic stabilization loop in the flight control system. As a result, some of the capability inherent in the X-29 was limited artificially by the system. And that was right, because no airplane had ever flown before with such a high degree of instability.

''So now we're looking to relax the conservatism and increase the ability of the pilot to get higher pitch rates (angles of attack) and higher G-onset rates. Then it will be more like a fighter. The roll rate, for example, was deliberately kept low to avoid inertial coupling. Missionized fighters have higher roll rates, and thus must accept the risk of inertial coupling.

''I believe the X-29 could approach the agility of the F-16 if we changed those current deliberate limitations (air vehicle number one). It would not become an operational fighter prototype, of course, but it would be more fighter-like than it has been allowed to be.

''There's been one big dividend from all our flight testing—we have advanced the technology of flight research. We learned how to flight-test a highly augmented vehicle and how to get real-time envelope-expansion data into the control room and the engineer's hands.''

### Guest Pilots

In addition to eight assigned X-29A-1 pilots, one Navy, five NASA, and six USAF pilots flew X-29A-1 during its program as guest pilots. Except for Navy Top Gun Lt. Cdr. Ray Craig (FIG. 6-7), who flew the airplane twice during Phase One, the NASA and USAF guest pilots flew it once apiece—all feeling a bit shortchanged. The five NASA jocks included William H. (Bill) Dana (FIG. 6-8), C. Gordon Fullerton (FIG. 6-9), Edward T. (Ed) Schneider (FIG. 6-10), Thomas C. (Tom) McMurtry (FIG. 6-11), and James W. (Jim) Smolka (FIG. 6-12). The six USAF guest pilots included Col. John M. Hoffman (FIG. 6-13), Col. David J. (Dave) McCloud (FIG. 6-14), Maj. Erwin B. (Bud) Jenschke (FIG. 6-15), Lt. Col. Jeffrey R. (Jeff) Riemer (FIG. 6-16), Lt. Col. Gregory V. Lewis (FIG. 6-17), and Maj. Dana D. Purifoy (FIG. 6-18).

*Fig. 6-8. William H. (Bill) Dana.*

*Fig. 6-7. Lt. Cdr. Ray Craig.*

*Fig. 6-9. C. Gordon Fullerton.*

*Fig. 6-10. Edward T. (Ed) Schneider.*

*Fig. 6-11. Thomas C. (Tom) McMurtry.*

*Fig. 6-12. James W. (Jim) Smolka.*

*Fig. 6-15.* *Maj. Erwin B. (Bud) Jenschke, Jr.*

*Fig. 6-13.* *Col. John M. Hoffman.*

*Fig. 6-14.* *Col. David J. (Dave) McCloud.*

*Fig. 6-16.* *Lt. Col. Jeffrey R. (Jeff) Riemer.*

*Fig. 6-17. Lt. Col. Gregory V. Lewis.*

*Fig. 6-18. Maj. Dana D. Purifoy.*

### John Hoffman

Even one flight on the X-29 leaves a lasting impression. Colonel Hoffman, Vice Commander of the AFFTC at Edwards AFB, who flew a single guest pilot sortie on X-29A-1, said: "My flight, one hour duration, was a technical evaluation of the X-29's performance and flying qualities. I was very impressed by both. The airplane handled very precisely and smoothly. And performance-wise, it was agile, powerful, and clean (little drag deceleration)."

### Ray Craig

Navy guest pilot Top Gun Ray Craig, who flew X-29A-1 from the USS *Edwards*, had this to say: "I only had those two flights, but I found the X-29 a lot more controllable and a lot more precise than I had expected. It's a very stable aircraft, despite the designed-in instability of 35 percent. You can put the airplane where you want it.

"And it's surprisingly easy to fly; by the second flight I was easily able to adapt to it, and I was able to hit the data points exactly. I flew it to a maximum of about 15 degrees angle of attack and rolled the wings with my feet off the rudder pedals. It wasn't high enough to see stall behavior, but it showed me that the lateral control hangs in up there (at 15 degrees AOA). And it seems to have potential for excellent sustained turn and turn-rate performance.

"I flew some simulated carrier approaches— not to touchdown, because the landing gear is not carrier-qualified— and there is no problem with pilot visibility in the landing attitude. And I did some air-to-ground tracking, simulating ordnance delivery."

Lt. Cdr. Craig was the only Navy pilot to fly X-29A-1. It is not known if a naval aviator will fly X-29A-2.

### David McCloud

Col. Dave McCloud, ex-Director of Advanced Programs for Tactical Air Command Headquarters, had one quest pilot flight on X-29A-1 and said: "I have had the opportunity to fly most fighter-type aircraft and feel very fortunate. As you well know, being in the right place at the right time has much to do with being selected for such activities. As Director of Advanced Programs for USAF/TAC [*he flew X-29A-1 during this assignment*], I found myself in a position where it was important for me to understand emerging technologies firsthand. The best way to do that is to fly an aircraft such as the X-29 if the system is that far along—thus the X-29, AV-8B, F-16 LANTIRN, and others. I've had other jobs of a similar nature in the past that opened doors like this. It's been extremely challenging, rewarding, and great fun!"

When asked to compare the X-29 with other aircraft he has flown, Col. McCloud said: "As to comparing the X-29 directly with the F-104, F-106, F-4, F-5 and other aircraft I've flown, I have some difficulty. First, the superb fly-by-wire flight control system of the X-29 masks some of the feel we had in the older systems. That is, the F-4, for example, felt big and solid. Given a fly-by-wire flight control system, you can make the aircraft feel any way you wish. Sometimes feel can give you wrong impressions when comparing aircraft. Secondly, it's been some time since I flew last generation aircraft and the memory is probably dulled, but I will try. Keep in mind that to really compare complex systems such as these, you must look at hard data including energy maneuverability diagrams.

"Overall, the X-29 seemed to hang on to energy (speed) better than other aircraft that I have flown. This seemed most apparent at the higher G-loads and angles of attack, where last generation aircraft were all, in a relative sense, energy losers. I felt that one of the high points of the X-29 was how far its flight control system had come in a short time. . .241 flights [*McCloud flew flight number 241 on X-29A number one*]. It was easy to transition to the X-29, and after 20 minutes I was comfortable, even at higher G-loads. This says a great deal for the quality engineers and test pilots that tuned this unique system. Both of the characteristics are very important to non-test pilots, i.e. operational fighter pilots. We are always looking for aircraft that sustain energy at high-G and high-AOA and that are easy to handle, especially at maximum performance. The X-29 fell into this category."

When asked "where to from here," Col. McCloud answered: "I believe it's important to finish the work on the X-29 program. A significant amount of money was spent to build the two aircraft and little will be required to complete the second phase of testing. I don't believe anybody knows where—or *if*—we will use the key features of the X-29 in the future. I believe that the next generation of fighter aircraft will be dominated in shape by the need for signature control (stealth), and that this requirement will exclude forward-swept wing design. If you look at the distinct shapes of the B-2 and F-117 you will understand what I mean. We will, however, certainly depend on fly-by-computer flight control systems. The F-16 led the way here and the operational guys are now not only believers but advocates."

### Jeff Riemer

Lt. Col. Jeff Riemer flew one guest pilot flight on X-29A-1 on 3 November 1988. He said of his flight preparation and flight: "My flight preparation time totalled about 14 hours—three hours of classroom time, two hours of individual instruction, three hours of simulator time, one hour of cockpit time, and five hours of self-study.

"Starting the aircraft and preparing for taxi (as the second pilot of the day) was very easy. During taxi the aircraft was content to go where it was pointed. It required low gain to taxi straight ahead (easier than a T-38).

"Takeoff acceleration in military thrust was average (about 3,500 feet for takeoff). Directional control was no problem with rudder only. I started aft stick pressure to rotate at 150 knots and stick forces and displacements were reasonable; however, the initial nose movement was more abrupt than expected. The nose movement was easy to stop, and there was no concern about getting airborne prematurely. I noticed a tendency to make extraneous inputs in roll during gear and flap retraction, which I expect is due to the light roll stick forces required. There were no undesirable pitch transients during gear and flap retraction. During touch-and-goes the abrupt nose movement wasn't noticeable. This may be due to the fact that the nosewheel is already off the ground, requiring less of an input.

"During flight it was very easy to accomplish a wings-level sideslip. Rudder forces were lighter than expected, and roll force required to hold the wings level was predictable. This was easier to do in the X-29 than in an F-4 or F-16.

"Capturing a desired bank angle was more difficult than captures in the pitch axis. I think the current roll rate (220 degrees per second) is the most that can be used effectively for small (less than 180 degrees) bank angle changes. Any faster and time would be wasted in stopping and capturing a desired condition, or the pilot would have a tendency to back off on the magnitude of the input to improve performance.

"Half and full-stick aileron rolls resulted in a large difference in roll rates. The half-stick roll rate was about one-third that of full-stick. I was not expecting the non-linear response, and the full deflection rate was a surprise; however, stopping the roll, in both cases, at the 360-degree point was easy.

"Pitch, yaw, and roll doublets at 15,000 feet and 300 knots damping was dead beat in all three axes.

"I flew the wind-up turn at 18,000 feet and 220 knots to 18 degrees AOA to investigate buffet and wing rock. Buffet was less than expected; however, controlling bank angle precisely would be difficult due to wing rock (five to 15 degrees). Stick force per G was linear.

"During landing, the aircraft was well-behaved during gear and flap extension with no undesirable transients. It was easy to hold a desired final turn airspeed of 165 knots and a final approach speed of 155 knots. The wind was strong and gusty, and the X-29 was very stable in the turbulence. I used the crabbed touchdown method for landing and feel the aricraft is easier to land in a crosswind than the F-16. Engine response (spool-up time) was not a problem. It was easy to hold the nose up on the touch-and-goes, and there was no tendency to over-rotate as power was applied. It felt very natural to land this aircraft even at the 15-knot crosswind limit."

Lt. Col. Riemer commented editorially as follows: "Why do we have aircraft like the X-29? It's not just so test pilots can have fun, although that's a nice spinoff; it's to demonstrate and explore new technologies that can be used in operational aircraft in the future. My 1.1 hour flight by no means allowed me to explore all the aircraft had to offer, but it did bring to light some possible applications for future use. Ten years ago, if I would have jumped in an aircraft with its wings on backwards and flown the profile I flew, the wings would have ripped off due to divergence. The accomplishments of being able to solve this problem with tailored composites will have far-reaching implications in the future.

"The canard has several possibilities; first, it appeared to greatly reduce motion of the crew station due to turbulence, and this makes it easier for a pilot to do his or her job, especially in the low level environment; secondly, as a flying surface it may have capabilities to control nose pointing at high angles of attack. It used to be that as aircraft reached areas of the flight envelope where stability derivatives went unstable, so did the aircraft. The X-29 has demonstrated that an aircraft which has a 35 percent negative static margin can be made to fly very respectably. We no longer have to build aircraft in conventional ways to obtain conventional flying characteristics, and this in itself is a great breakthrough. With supersonic cruise becoming a high-interest item, I can't help but think the reduced transonic drag demonstrated by the X-29 will be applicable to future programs. The upcoming high AOA program will also produce necessary information to allow us to move forward in the area of advanced maneuvering. We need the X-29 program and future X programs to advance the way we think about solving problems to better utilize the capabilities of airpower."

In a nutshell, then, each X-29 pilot who shared his comments has either praised or faulted the aircraft (FIG. 6-19). The former comments far outweigh the latter. Thus the Grumman X-29A Forward-Swept Wing Advanced Technology Demonstrator is a bona fide success. What more can be said of an airplane—*especially* an X airplane?

**Fig. 6-19.** *Maj. Alan D. (Al) Hoover, X-29A Program Manager and Test Pilot.*

# Conclusions

WHAT BEGAN as a private individual's research effort to obtain a Ph.D. in aeronautical engineering dramatically metamorphosed into one of aviation history's most rewarding aircraft programs—the DARPA/NASA/USAF-sponsored Grumman X-29A Forward-Swept Wing Advanced Technology Demonstrator—the first X-type aircraft to fly in some 10 years. It is a story that cannot yet be concluded, although the program is already some 16 years old.

The two X-29s are not only unique in design, but they proved that they could perform their role—specifically, to maneuver in the transonic regime and at high angles of bank and attack, without stalling and falling, flight after flight. The forward-swept wing works.

Both aircraft have flown on a regular basis without any major discrepancies or required aerodynamic design changes. The X-29A has proved the safest X airplane ever flown, and with turnaround times comparable to missionized fighters.

Continuing its flights to higher and higher angles of attack—most probably to 90 degrees before returning permanently to a zero angle of attack for retirement—the number two X-29A is still an active entity of America's endless quest for advanced flying capabilities.

The X-29 and its advanced technologies are proof that mankind, in the search for better ways to fly, has not stagnated. It might just be that now the birds are watching *us*.

# Postscript

FOLLOWING flight number 44 on 30 May 1990, the number two X-29A was housed in its NASA hanger. After that action, selected parts were removed from the airplane for installation on the number one X-29A so that it could be shown and flown at some air shows, including Dayton and Oshkosh. At the time, X-29A number two was scheduled to fly again in October 1990, pending funding of flight 45. During flight number 44 the X-29A-2 airplane attained a Mach number of 0.69 and a 17° AOA at 30,700 feet. Flight duration was 0.8 hours, totaling 39.4 flight hours.

To the best of my knowledge, the appearance of the X-29 at 1990 air shows is a first. Apparently there is a great deal of confidence in the capabilities of the X-29 airplane.

# X-29A Pilots and Personnel

## X-29A-1 Assigned and Guest Pilots

| Name | Number of Flights | Organization & Title of Pilot |
|------|-------------------|-------------------------------|
| Stephen D. (Steve) Ishmael | 63 | NASA X-29A   Project Pilot |
| Rogers E. Smith | 56 | NASA X-29A   Co-Project Pilot |
| Lt. Col. Harry C. Walker III | 33 | Former AFFTC X-29A   Program Manager/Test Pilot |
| Maj. Alan D. (Al) Hoover | 25 | Former AFFTC X-29A   Program Manager/Test Pilot |
| Kurt C. Shroeder | 23 | Former Grumman X-29A   Co-Project Pilot/Project Pilot |
| Rod (Rocket) Womer | 14 | Grumman X-29A   Project Pilot |
| Col. Theodore J. (Ted) Wierzbanowski | 10 | Former AFFTC X-29A   Program Manager/Test Pilot (first) |
| Charles A. (Chuck) Sewell | 5 | Grumman X-29A   Chief Project Pilot |
| Lt. Cmdr. Ray Craig | 2 | USN X-29A   Guest Pilot |
| C. Gordon Fullerton | 1 | NASA X-29A   Guest Pilot |
| William H. (Bill) Dana | 1 | NASA X-29A   Guest Pilot |
| Thomas C. (Tom) McMurtry | 1 | NASA X-29A   Guest Pilot |
| James W. (Jim) Smolka | 1 | NASA X-29A   Guest Pilot |
| Edward T. (Ed) Schneider | 1 | NASA X-29A   Guest Pilot |

| Name | Number of Flights | Organization & Title of Pilot | |
|------|------------------|-----------------|---|
| Col. David J. (Dave) McCloud | 1 | USAF X-29A | Guest Pilot |
| Col. John M. Hoffman | 1 | USAF X-29A | Guest Pilot/AFFTC Vice Commander |
| Lt. Col. Jeffrey R. (Jeff) Riemer | 1 | USAF X-29A | Guest Pilot |
| Lt. Col. Erwin B. (Bud) Jenschke, Jr. | 1 | USAF X-29A | Guest Pilot |
| Lt. Col. Gregory V. (Greg) Lewis | 1 | USAF X-29A | Guest Pilot |
| Maj. Dana D. Purifoy | 1 | USAF X-29A | Guest Pilot/Current AFFTC X-29A Program Manager/Test Pilot |
| | 242 | Total Flights | |

## X-29A-2 Assigned and Guest Pilots

| Name | Number of Flights | Organization & Title of Pilot | |
|------|------------------|-----------------|---|
| Stephen D. (Steve) Ishmael | 9 | NASA X-29A | Project Pilot |
| Rogers E. Smith | 8 | NASA X-29A | Co-Project Pilot |
| Rod (Rocket) Womer | 6 | Grumman X-29A | Project Pilot |
| Maj. Alan D. (Al) Hoover | 7 | Former AFFTC X-29A | Program Manager/Test Pilot |
| Maj. Dana D. Purifoy | 4 | Current AFFTC X-29A | Program Manager/Test Pilot |

*As of 11 April 1990.

# X-29A Program and Project Directors and Managers (partial)

| Name & Title | Organization and Duration | | |
|---|---|---|---|
| Robert L. (Bob) Roemer<br>*Program Director* | Grumman<br>80–85 | Walter J. (Wally) Sefic<br>*Project Manager* | NASA<br>82–86 |
| John Calandra<br>*Program Director* | Grumman<br>85–87 | Gary A. Trippensee<br>*Project Manager* | NASA<br>86– |
| William Mebes<br>*Program Director* | Grumman<br>87–89 | Col. Norris J. Krone, Jr.<br>*Program Manager* | DARPA<br>76–80 |
| Thomas A. (Tom) Taglarine<br>*Program Director* | Grumman<br>89– | Col. James N. (Jim) Allburn<br>*Program Manager* | DARPA<br>80– |
| Glenn L. Spacht<br>*Deputy Program Director* | Grumman<br>76–85 | Col. James (Jim) Wansack<br>*Program Manager* | USAF |
| Terry Putnam<br>*Project Manager* | NASA<br>80–82 | | |

# Flight Log

## X-29A-1

| Flight Number | Date | Duration in Hours | Maximum Altitude | Maximum Mach | Pilot & Organization | |
|---|---|---|---|---|---|---|
| 1[1] | 12-14-84 | 1.1 | 15,000 | 0.43 | Sewell | Grumman |
| 2 | 02-04-85 | 1.3 | 15,000 | 0.56 | Sewell | Grumman |
| 3 | 02-22-85 | 1.4 | 15,000 | 0.61 | Sewell | Grumman |
| 4[2] | 03-01-85 | 1.1 | 15,000 | 0.60 | Schroeder | Grumman |
| 5[3] | 04-02-85 | 1.4 | 15,310 | 0.55 | Ishmael | NASA |
| 6[4] | 04-04-85 | 1.4 | 15,516 | 0.57 | Wierzbanowski | USAF |
| 7 | 04-09-85 | 1.5 | 20,120 | 0.60 | Smith | NASA |
| 8 | 04-16-85 | 1.8 | 20,376 | 0.62 | Sewell | Grumman |
| 9 | 05-21-85 | 1.4 | 30,188 | 0.61 | Schroeder | Grumman |
| 10 | 05-29-85 | 1.2 | 31,237 | 0.60 | Ishmael | NASA |
| 11 | 05-29-85 | 1.4 | 30,861 | 0.60 | Wierzbanowski | USAF |
| 12 | 06-06-85 | 1.3 | 30,861 | 0.61 | Smith | NASA |
| 13 | 06-06-85 | 1.1 | 20,200 | 0.56 | Schroeder | Grumman |
| 14 | 06-11-85 | 1.2 | 16,108 | 0.62 | Ishmael | NASA |

| Flight Number | Date | Duration in Hours | Maximum Altitude | Maximum Mach | Pilot & Organization | |
|---|---|---|---|---|---|---|
| 15 | 06-11-85 | 1.4 | 30,228 | 0.58 | Sewell | Grumman |
| 16 | 06-13-85 | 1.2 | 25,374 | 0.61 | Wierzbanowski | USAF |
| 17 | 08-14-85 | 1.5 | 30,000 | 0.70 | Smith | NASA |
| 18 | 08-22-85 | 1.3 | 30,000 | 0.75 | Schroeder | Grumman |
| 19 | 08-22-85 | 1.2 | 30,000 | 0.70 | Ishmael | NASA |
| 20 | 11-01-85 | 1.5 | 40,904 | 0.80 | Wierzbanowski | USAF |
| 21 | 11-07-85 | 1.4 | 40,373 | 0.79 | Ishmael | NASA |
| 22 | 11-19-85 | 1.0 | 40,308 | 0.83 | Smith | NASA |
| 23 | 11-20-85 | 0.8 | 40,561 | 0.83 | Schroeder | Grumman |
| 24 | 11-27-85 | 1.5 | 40,000 | 0.90 | Smith | NASA |
| 25 | 12-06-85 | 1.4 | 41,113 | 0.94 | Wierzbanowski | USAF |
| 26[5] | 12-13-85 | 1.0 | 40,000 | 1.03 | Ishmael | NASA |
| 27 | 12-20-85 | 1.0 | 40,000 | 1.07 | Schroeder | Grumman |
| 28 | 12-20-85 | 1.0 | 40,000 | 1.10 | Wierzbanowski | USAF |
| 29 | 12-20-85 | 1.6 | 40,000 | 0.95 | Smith | NASA |
| 30 | 01-15-86 | 0.3 | 9,800 | 0.40 | Ishmael | NASA |
| 31 | 01-23-86 | 1.3 | 30,000 | 0.85 | Schroeder | Grumman |
| 32 | 01-23-86 | 0.7 | 40,000 | 1.20 | Wierzbanowski | USAF |
| 33 | 02-07-86 | 1.0 | 40,000 | 1.10 | Smith | NASA |
| 34 | 02-07-86 | 1.0 | 30,000 | 0.85 | Ishmael | NASA |
| 35 | 02-19-86 | 0.7 | 15,000 | 0.60 | Ishmael | NASA |
| 36 | 02-21-86 | 1.3 | 40,000 | 1.12 | Ishmael | NASA |
| 37 | 02-21-86 | 1.4 | 30,000 | 0.73 | Ishmael | NASA |
| 38 | 02-27-86 | 1.2 | 40,000 | 1.05 | Smith | NASA |
| 39 | 02-27-86 | 1.1 | 40,000 | 1.10 | Wierzbanowski | USAF |
| 40 | 06-10-86 | 1.2 | 40,000 | 0.95 | Schroeder | Grumman |
| 41 | 06-12-86 | 0.7 | 20,000 | 0.55 | Ishmael | NASA |
| 42 | 06-12-86 | 1.2 | 30,000 | 0.95 | Ishmael | NASA |
| 43 | 06-12-86 | 0.8 | 40,000 | 1.30 | Smith | NASA |
| 44 | 06-12-86 | 0.7 | 40,000 | 1.30 | Wierzbanowski | USAF |
| 45 | 07-11-86 | 1.0 | 40,000 | 0.95 | Schroeder | Grumman |
| 46 | 07-15-86 | 1.1 | 40,000 | 1.20 | Wierzbanowski | USAF |
| 47 | 07-15-86 | 0.7 | 40,000 | 1.40 | Smith | NASA |
| 48 | 07-18-86 | 0.8 | 30,000 | 1.05 | Ishmael | NASA |
| 49 | 07-18-86 | 1.0 | 30,000 | 1.10 | Walker | USAF |

| Flight Number | Date | Duration in Hours | Maximum Altitude | Maximum Mach | Pilot & Organization | |
|---|---|---|---|---|---|---|
| 50 | 07-18-86 | 0.7 | 40,000 | 1.30 | Smith | NASA |
| 51 | 07-24-86 | 0.9 | 40,000 | 1.20 | Schroeder | Grumman |
| 52 | 07-24-86 | 0.5 | 20,000 | 0.90 | Ishmael | NASA |
| 53 | 07-30-86 | 0.7 | 30,000 | 1.20 | Walker | USAF |
| 54 | 07-30-86 | 0.7 | 30,000 | 1.20 | Smith | NASA |
| 55 | 07-30-86 | 0.7 | 30,000 | 1.30 | Schroeder | Grumman |
| 56 | 08-01-86 | 0.5 | 30,000 | 1.30 | Ishmael | NASA |
| 57 | 08-01-86 | 0.5 | 30,000 | 1.30 | Schroeder | Grumman |
| 58 | 08-01-86 | 0.5 | 30,000 | 1.20 | Ishmael | NASA |
| 59 | 08-08-86 | 0.6 | 20,000 | 1.03 | Smith | NASA |
| 60 | 08-08-86 | 0.5 | 20,000 | 1.10 | Schroeder | Grumman |
| 61 | 08-08-86 | 0.5 | 20,000 | 1.10 | Ishmael | NASA |
| 62 | 08-08-86 | 0.4 | 20,000 | 1.175 | Smith | NASA |
| 63 | 08-13-86 | 0.7 | 30,000 | 1.20 | Schroeder | Grumman |
| 64 | 08-13-86 | 0.6 | 25,000 | 1.20 | Ishmael | NASA |
| 65 | 08-13-86 | 0.6 | 25,000 | 1.20 | Smith | NASA |
| 66 | 08-27-86 | 0.9 | 30,000 | 0.925 | Walker | USAF |
| 67 | 08-27-86 | 0.6 | 40,000 | 0.90 | Schroeder | Grumman |
| 68 | 08-27-86 | 0.9 | 15,000 | 0.90 | Schroeder | Grumman |
| 69 | 08-27-86 | 0.8 | 15,000 | 0.85 | Ishmael | NASA |
| 70 | 09-05-86 | 0.7 | 15,000 | 0.97 | Smith | NASA |
| 71 | 09-05-86 | 0.9 | 20,000 | 0.97 | Walker | USAF |
| 72 | 10-24-86 | 0.6 | 30,000 | 1.03 | Schroeder | Grumman |
| 73 | 10-29-86 | 0.5 | 15,000 | 1.10 | Ishmael | NASA |
| 74 | 10-29-86 | 0.5 | 30,000 | 1.10 | Smith | NASA |
| 75 | 10-29-86 | 0.7 | 34,000 | 0.90 | Walker | USAF |
| 76 | 10-29-86 | 0.4 | 15,000 | 1.16 | Ishmael | NASA |
| 77 | 11-07-86 | 0.7 | 43,000 | 0.95 | Schroeder | Grumman |
| 78 | 11-07-86 | 0.7 | 34,000 | 0.97 | Smith | NASA |
| 79 | 11-07-86 | 0.5 | 8,000 | 1.03 | Walker | USAF |
| 80 | 11-07-86 | 0.4 | 10,000 | 1.05 | Ishmael | NASA |
| 81 | 11-14-86 | 0.4 | 10,000 | 1.12 | Schroeder | Grumman |
| 82 | 11-14-86 | 0.4 | 10,000 | 1.10 | Smith | NASA |
| 83 | 11-14-86 | 1.0 | 20,000 | — | Walker | USAF |
| 84 | 11-14-86 | 1.0 | 20,000 | — | Ishmael | NASA |

| Flight Number | Date | Duration in Hours | Maximum Altitude | Maximum Mach | Pilot & Organization | |
|---|---|---|---|---|---|---|
| 85 | 11-19-86 | 0.4 | 15,000 | 1.05 | Walker | USAF |
| 86 | 11-19-86 | 0.5 | 10,000 | 1.05 | Ishmael | NASA |
| 87 | 11-19-86 | 0.5 | 22,000 | 1.20 | Walker | USAF |
| 88 | 12-03-86 | 1.0 | 20,000 | — | Schroeder | Grumman |
| 89 | 12-03-86 | 0.6 | 45,000 | 1.20 | Ishmael | NASA |
| 90 | 12-03-86 | 1.1 | 20,000 | — | Smith | NASA |
| 91 | 12-05-86 | 0.6 | 41,700 | 1.33 | Walker | USAF |
| 92 | 12-05-86 | 0.8 | 45,300 | 1.02 | Smith | NASA |
| 93 | 12-05-86 | 0.5 | 39,200 | 1.27 | Ishmael | NASA |
| 94 | 12-05-86 | 0.8 | 25,900 | 1.09 | Schroeder | Grumman |
| 95 | 12-10-86 | 0.5 | 41,100 | 1.43 | Walker | USAF |
| 96 | 12-10-86 | 0.6 | 36,200 | 1.29 | Schroeder | Grumman |
| 97 | 12-12-86 | 0.5 | 22,000 | 1.20 | Ishmael | NASA |
| 98 | 12-12-86 | 0.6 | 18,000 | 1.10 | Smith | NASA |
| 99 | 12-17-86 | 0.6 | 47,600 | 1.45 | Walker | USAF |
| 100 | 12-17-86 | 0.6 | 50,200 | 1.46 | Ishmael | NASA |
| 101 | 12-17-86 | 0.7 | 20,000 | 0.9 | Smith | NASA |
| 102 | 12-23-86 | 0.8 | 30,300 | 1.0 | Walker | USAF |
| 103 | 12-23-86 | 1.1 | 22,300 | 0.8 | Craig | USN |
| 104[6] | 12-23-86 | 1.5 | 15,500 | 0.7 | Craig | USN |
| 105[7] | 06-19-87 | 0.8 | 39,500 | 1.27 | Ishmael | NASA |
| 106 | 06-26-87 | 0.7 | 31,500 | 0.996 | Walker | USAF |
| 107 | 06-26-87 | 0.9 | 46,100 | 1.39 | Ishmael | NASA |
| 108 | 06-26-87 | 0.8 | 30,300 | 1.10 | Walker | USAF |
| 109 | 06-30-87 | 0.7 | 31,700 | 0.985 | Smith | NASA |
| 110 | 06-30-87 | 0.8 | 45,150 | 1.35 | Ishmael | NASA |
| 111 | 07-24-87 | 0.7 | 46,100 | 1.01 | Schroeder | Grumman |
| 112 | 07-24-87 | 0.5 | 35,970 | 1.22 | Walker | USAF |
| 113 | 07-24-87 | 0.6 | 25,039 | 0.91 | Smith | NASA |
| 114 | 07-29-87 | 0.4 | 20,280 | 1.17 | Ishmael | NASA |
| 115 | 07-29-87 | 0.7 | 15,080 | 0.925 | Walker | USAF |
| 116 | 08-05-87 | 0.9 | 42,512 | 0.94 | Smith | NASA |
| 117 | 08-05-87 | 0.6 | 27,300 | 0.95 | Ishmael | NASA |
| 118 | 08-05-87 | 0.6 | 33,128 | 0.95 | Walker | USAF |
| 119 | 08-07-87 | 0.5 | 12,616 | 1.05 | Smith | NASA |

| Flight Number | Date | Duration in Hours | Maximum Altitude | Maximum Mach | Pilot & Organization | |
|---|---|---|---|---|---|---|
| 120 | 08-19-87 | 0.4 | 43,677 | 1.24 | Ishmael | NASA |
| 121[8] | 08-19-87 | 0.6 | 50,707 | 1.21 | Walker | USAF |
| 122 | 08-19-87 | 0.5 | 37,927 | 1.21 | Smith | NASA |
| 123 | 08-19-87 | 0.4 | 33,178 | 1.23 | Ishmael | NASA |
| 124 | 09-09-87 | 0.7 | 32,287 | 0.94 | Walker | USAF |
| 125 | 09-09-87 | 0.6 | 38,180 | 1.31 | Ishmael | NASA |
| 126 | 09-11-87 | 0.5 | 32,432 | 1.13 | Walker | USAF |
| 127 | 09-11-87 | 1.1 | 33,596 | 0.92 | Ishmael | NASA |
| 128 | 09-11-87 | 0.7 | 25,585 | 1.21 | Walker | USAF |
| 129 | 09-11-87 | 0.9 | 43,339 | 1.01 | Ishmael | NASA |
| 130 | 10-09-87 | 0.6 | 30,853 | 1.33 | Walker | USAF |
| 131 | 10-09-87 | 0.4 | 31,399 | 1.33 | Ishmael | NASA |
| 132 | 10-09-87 | 0.6 | 17,325 | 1.08 | Walker | USAF |
| 133 | 10-09-87 | 0.4 | 20,415 | 1.09 | Ishmael | NASA |
| 134 | 10-14-87 | 0.7 | 39,505 | 0.97 | Walker | USAF |
| 135 | 10-14-87 | 0.8 | 44,561 | 0.96 | Ishmael | NASA |
| 136 | 10-14-87 | 0.6 | 40,174 | 1.01 | Walker | USAF |
| 137 | 10-16-87 | 0.6 | 31,221 | 0.99 | Ishmael | NASA |
| 138 | 10-16-87 | 0.7 | 39,305 | 1.13 | Walker | USAF |
| 139 | 10-16-87 | 0.4 | 44,815 | 1.12 | Ishmael | NASA |
| 140 | 11-04-87 | 0.9 | 38,489 | 0.98 | Smith | NASA |
| 141 | 11-06-87 | 0.5 | 37,656 | 1.27 | Walker | USAF |
| 142 | 11-06-87 | 0.8 | 40,752 | 1.04 | Ishmael | NASA |
| 143 | 11-18-87 | 0.7 | 35,929 | 0.96 | Smith | NASA |
| 144 | 11-18-87 | 0.8 | 33,692 | 0.96 | Walker | NASA |
| 145 | 11-18-87 | 0.8 | 35,146 | 0.95 | Dana | NASA |
| 146 | 12-02-87 | 0.7 | 34,325 | 0.96 | Ishmael | NASA |
| 147[9] | 12-04-87 | 0.6 | 40,461 | 1.48 | Walker | USAF |
| 148 | 12-04-87 | 0.9 | 40,802 | 1.06 | Womer | Grumman |
| 149 | 12-09-87 | 0.6 | 33,245 | 1.01 | Ishmael | NASA |
| 150 | 12-09-87 | 0.6 | 49,564 | 1.33 | Walker | USAF |
| 151 | 12-09-87 | 0.6 | 34,873 | 1.31 | Womer | Grumman |
| 152 | 12-11-87 | 0.8 | 40,822 | 0.99 | Ishmael | NASA |
| 153 | 12-11-87 | 0.6 | 46,971 | 1.31 | Walker | USAF |
| 154 | 12-11-87 | 1.0 | 30,739 | 1.21 | Smolka | NASA |

| Flight Number | Date | Duration in Hours | Maximum Altitude | Maximum Mach | Pilot & Organization | |
|---|---|---|---|---|---|---|
| 155 | 12-18-87 | 0.8 | 31,594 | 0.96 | Smith | NASA |
| 156 | 01-08-88 | 0.6 | 22,437 | 0.98 | Ishmael | NASA |
| 157 | 01-13-88 | 0.8 | 31,425 | 0.96 | Womer | Grumman |
| 158 | 01-13-88 | 0.7 | 30,562 | 0.95 | Smith | NASA |
| 159 | 01-13-88 | 0.5 | 30,199 | 1.02 | Hoover | USAF |
| 160 | 01-22-88 | 0.7 | 31,889 | 1.03 | Walker | USAF |
| 161 | 01-22-88 | 0.8 | 32,662 | 1.01 | Hoover | USAF |
| 162 | 01-22-88 | 0.7 | 26,937 | 1.16 | Womer | Grumman |
| 163 | 01-27-88 | 0.9 | 37,589 | 0.94 | Smith | NASA |
| 164 | 01-27-88 | 0.8 | 35,391 | 0.96 | Smith | NASA |
| 165 | 02-05-88 | 0.2 | 26,201 | 0.96 | Ishmael | NASA |
| 166 | 02-12-88 | 0.7 | 30,307 | 0.94 | Hoover | USAF |
| 167 | 02-12-88 | 0.6 | 32,924 | 1.24 | Ishmael | NASA |
| 168 | 02-12-88 | 0.7 | 38,315 | 1.04 | McMurtry | NASA |
| 169 | 03-16-88 | 0.7 | 31,223 | 0.97 | Smith | NASA |
| 170 | 03-16-88 | 0.6 | 42,983 | 1.18 | Hoover | USAF |
| 171 | 03-16-88 | 1.0 | 26,399 | 0.91 | Schneider | NASA |
| 172 | 03-23-88 | 0.7 | 44,348 | 1.11 | Womer | Grumman |
| 173 | 03-23-88 | 0.6 | 36,789 | 1.23 | Ishmael | NASA |
| 174 | 03-23-88 | 0.6 | 34,406 | 1.21 | Hoover | USAF |
| 175 | 03-30-88 | 0.5 | 50,390 | 1.27 | Womer | Grumman |
| 176 | 03-30-88 | 0.5 | 48,883 | 1.26 | Ishmael | NASA |
| 177 | 03-30-88 | 0.5 | 33,799 | 1.20 | Womer | Grumman |
| 178 | 04-06-88 | 0.5 | 48,398 | 1.21 | Smith | NASA |
| 179 | 04-06-88 | 0.6 | 46,670 | 1.27 | Hoover | USAF |
| 180 | 04-06-88 | 0.6 | 26,674 | 1.22 | Ishmael | NASA |
| 181 | 04-13-88 | 0.7 | 17,824 | 0.89 | Womer | Grumman |
| 182 | 04-15-88 | 0.5 | 32,591 | 1.22 | Hoover | USAF |
| 183 | 04-22-88 | 0.7 | 26,719 | 0.87 | Ishmael | NASA |
| 184 | 04-22-88 | 0.5 | 36,205 | 1.21 | Smith | NASA |
| 185 | 04-22-88 | 1.0 | 31,081 | 1.08 | Fullerton | NASA |
| 186 | 04-22-88 | 0.5 | 41,683 | 1.26 | Hoover | USAF |
| 187 | 05-20-88 | 0.5 | 33,522 | 1.24 | Ishmael | NASA |
| 188 | 05-20-88 | 0.5 | 28,271 | 1.22 | Smith | NASA |
| 189 | 05-20-88 | 0.4 | 28,688 | 1.21 | Hoover | USAF |

| Flight Number | Date | Duration in Hours | Maximum Altitude | Maximum Mach | Pilot & Organization | |
|---|---|---|---|---|---|---|
| 190 | 05-20-88 | 0.3 | 30,320 | 1.31 | Ishmael | NASA |
| 191 | 05-25-88 | 0.5 | 24,808 | 1.05 | Smith | NASA |
| 192 | 05-25-88 | 0.6 | 46,243 | 1.29 | Ishmael | NASA |
| 193 | 05-25-88 | 0.4 | 29,849 | 1.21 | Smith | NASA |
| 194 | 06-01-88 | 0.7 | 35,551 | 1.07 | Hoover | USAF |
| 195 | 06-01-88 | 0.7 | 37,530 | 1.06 | Ishmael | NASA |
| 196 | 06-01-88 | 0.6 | 27,610 | 1.21 | Hoover | USAF |
| 197 | 06-08-88 | 0.8 | 29,788 | 0.96 | Smith | NASA |
| 198 | 06-08-88 | 0.8 | 26,078 | 0.98 | Ishmael | NASA |
| 199 | 06-08-88 | 0.8 | 31,336 | 0.97 | Hoover | USAF |
| 200[10] | 06-08-88 | 0.6 | 46,225 | 1.23 | Smith | NASA |
| 201 | 07-06-88 | 0.5 | 32,992 | 1.03 | Womer | Grumman |
| 202 | 07-06-88 | 0.4 | 20,354 | 1.03 | Hoover | USAF |
| 203 | 07-06-88 | 0.7 | 37,102 | 0.96 | Smith | NASA |
| 204 | 07-13-88 | 0.6 | 22,977 | 0.96 | Womer | Grumman |
| 205 | 07-13-88 | 0.8 | 31,242 | 0.94 | Hoover | USAF |
| 206 | 07-13-88 | 0.6 | 31,598 | 1.20 | Smith | NASA |
| 207 | 07-22-88 | 0.6 | 21,623 | 1.01 | Ishmael | NASA |
| 208 | 07-22-88 | 0.9 | 23,713 | 0.82 | Lewis | USAF |
| 209 | 07-22-88 | 0.8 | 21,575 | 1.01 | Smith | NASA |
| 210 | 07-27-88 | 0.4 | 15,397 | 0.57 | Womer | Grumman |
| 211 | 07-27-88 | 1.1 | 17,061 | 0.78 | Hoover | USAF |
| 212 | 07-27-88 | 0.9 | 21,904 | 0.77 | Jenschke | USAF |
| 213 | 07-27-88 | 0.7 | 20,688 | 0.68 | Smith | NASA |
| 214 | 10-06-88 | 1.0 | 30,580 | 0.63 | Hoover | USAF |
| 215 | 10-12-88 | 1.0 | 16,411 | 0.81 | Smith | NASA |
| 216 | 10-12-88 | 0.8 | 16,441 | 0.92 | Womer | Grumman |
| 217 | 10-12-88 | 1.0 | 22,518 | 0.96 | Smith | NASA |
| 218 | 10-18-88 | 0.6 | 21,250 | 0.96 | Hoover | USAF |
| 219 | 10-18-88 | 0.8 | 20,223 | 0.90 | Smith | NASA |
| 220 | 10-18-88 | 0.8 | 20,587 | 0.96 | Hoover | USAF |
| 221 | 10-20-88 | 0.7 | 40,006 | 0.97 | Womer | Grumman |
| 222 | 10-20-88 | 0.8 | 16,982 | 0.87 | Hoover | USAF |
| 223 | 11-03-88 | 0.8 | 21,404 | 0.95 | Smith | NASA |
| 224 | 11-03-88 | 1.0 | 23,432 | 0.85 | Riemer | USAF |

| Flight Number | Date | Duration in Hours | Maximum Altitude | Maximum Mach | Pilot & Organization | |
|---|---|---|---|---|---|---|
| 225 | 11-03-88 | 0.9 | 20,804 | 0.88 | Womer | Grumman |
| 226[11] | 11-09-88 | 0.4 | 12,235 | 1.11 | Hoover | USAF |
| 227 | 11-09-88 | 0.6 | 32,457 | 1.04 | Smith | NASA |
| 228 | 11-09-88 | 0.6 | 40,518 | 1.26 | Hoover | USAF |
| 229 | 11-09-88 | 0.8 | 20,295 | 0.88 | Smith | NASA |
| 230 | 11-15-88 | 0.8 | 21,292 | 0.86 | Hoover | USAF |
| 231 | 11-15-88 | 0.9 | 19,602 | 0.81 | Smith | NASA |
| 232 | 11-15-88 | 0.8 | 20,570 | 0.96 | Hoover | USAF |
| 233 | 11-18-88 | 0.5 | 41,675 | 1.21 | Smith | NASA |
| 234 | 11-18-88 | 1.0 | 22,720 | 0.92 | Purifoy | USAF |
| 235 | 11-18-88 | 0.8 | 24,060 | 0.89 | Hoover | USAF |
| 236 | 11-23-88 | 0.8 | 20,599 | 0.87 | Ishmael | NASA |
| 237 | 11-23-88 | 0.9 | 23,402 | 0.84 | Smith | NASA |
| 238 | 11-23-88 | 0.5 | 26,892 | 1.21 | Hoover | USAF |
| 239[12] | 12-08-88 | 0.5 | 32,527 | 1.01 | Ishmael | NASA |
| 240 | 12-08-88 | 0.9 | 25,611 | 0.84 | Hoffman | USAF |
| 241 | 12-08-88 | 0.8 | 20,838 | 0.92 | McCloud | USAF |
| 242 | 12-08-88 | 0.5 | 33,163 | 0.97 | Smith | NASA |

**Total Flight Time:** 178.5 hours

[1]First contractor evaluation flight.

[2]Last contractor evaluation flight.

[3]First government Phase One flight; first NASA flight.

[4]First USAF flight.

[5]First supersonic flight of a forward-swept wing aircraft.

[6]Last government Phase One flight.

[7]First government Phase Two flight.

[8]50,707 feet; altitude record.

[9]Mach 1.48; speed record.

[10]200th flight; number record for X-type aircraft.

[11]New airspeed record of 665 KEAS (1.10 Mach/5,032 feet) was attained.

[12]New negative load factor of $-1.9$g (equivalent) and angle-of-attack of $-4.2$ degrees were attained at 0.60 Mach/10,000 feet; new positive load factor of 6.7G (equivalent) was attained at 0.95 Mach/20,600 feet.

# X-29A-2

| Flight Number | Date | Duration in Hours | Maximum Altitude | Maximum Mach | Pilot & Organization | |
|---|---|---|---|---|---|---|
| 1 | 05-23-89 | 0.9 | 28,500 | 0.60 | Ishmael | NASA |
| 2 | 06-13-89 | 0.9 | 30,000 | 0.95 | Hoover | USAF |
| 3 | 06-13-89 | 1.1 | 25,000 | 0.80 | Ishmael | NASA |
| 4 | 06-23-89 | 1.0 | 30,000 | 0.63 | Hoover | USAF |
| 5 | 06-23-89 | 1.1 | 30,000 | 0.85 | Smith | NASA |
| 6 | 10-11-89 | 0.9 | 20,000 | 0.81 | Womer | Grumman |
| 7 | 10-11-89 | 0.9 | 30,000 | 0.93 | Ishmael | NASA |
| 8 | 10-19-89 | 1.0 | 37,200 | 0.54 | Hoover | USAF |
| 9 | 11-08-89 | 1.0 | 35,000 | — | Smith | NASA |
| 10[1] | 11-08-89 | 1.1 | 36,000 | — | Womer | Grumman |
| 11[2] | 11-28-89 | 0.7 | 39,000 | — | Ishmael | NASA |
| 12[3] | 12-19-89 | 0.9 | 37,900 | — | Hoover | USAF |
| 13[4] | 01-04-90 | 0.7 | 38,400 | — | Smith | NASA |
| 14 | 01-04-90 | 0.9 | 37,900 | — | Womer | Grumman |
| 15[5] | 01-11-90 | 0.9 | 39,700 | 0.57 | Ishmael | NASA |
| 16[6] | 01-25-90 | 0.9 | 37,700 | — | Hoover | USAF |
| 17 | 01-25-90 | 1.0 | 36,800 | — | Smith | NASA |
| 18[7] | 01-25-90 | 1.1 | 38,000 | 0.70 | Purifoy | USAF |
| 19[8] | 02-01-90 | 0.8 | 39,000 | 0.72 | Womer | Grumman |
| 20 | 02-08-90 | 0.9 | 37,300 | — | Ishmael | NASA |
| 21 | 02-08-90 | 1.1 | 36,100 | — | Hoover | USAF |
| 22 | 02-08-90 | 1.1 | 35,800 | — | Smith | NASA |
| 23[9] | 02-15-90 | 1.0 | 35,700 | — | Smith | NASA |
| 24[10] | 02-15-90 | 0.9 | 35,300 | — | Hoover | USAF |
| 25 | 02-15-90 | 0.9 | 37,500 | — | Purifoy | USAF |
| 26 | 03-09-90 | 0.7 | 35,800 | 0.60 | Ishmael | NASA |
| 27[11] | 03-09-90 | 0.4 | 38,400 | — | Womer | Grumman |
| 28 | 03-09-90 | 1.0 | 41,300 | — | Smith | NASA |
| 29 | 03-22-90 | 0.9 | 36,200 | — | Purifoy | USAF |
| 30 | 03-22-90 | 1.0 | 40,000 | — | Ishmael | NASA |
| 31[12] | 03-22-90 | — | — | — | Smith | NASA |
| 31[13] | 03-29-90 | 1.0 | 41,600 | 0.92 | Womer | Grumman |
| 32 | 03-29-90 | 0.9 | 40,100 | — | Smith | NASA |

| Flight Number | Date | Duration in Hours | Maximum Altitude | Maximum Mach | Pilot & Organization | |
|---|---|---|---|---|---|---|
| 33 | 03-29-90 | 0.9 | 38,100 | — | Purifoy | USAF |
| 34[14] | 04-06-90 | — | — | — | Ishmael | NASA |
| 34 | 04-11-90 | 0.8 | 37,100 | 0.30 | Ishmael | NASA |
| 35[15] | 04-11-90 | — | — | — | Womer | Grumman |
| 35[16] | 04-17-90 | 0.5 | 38,000 | — | Smith | NASA |
| 36 | 04-17-90 | 0.9 | 41,800 | — | Womer | Grumman |
| 37[17] | 04-17-90 | 0.7 | 35,100 | — | Purifoy | USAF |
| 38 | 04-27-90 | 0.8 | 38,000 | — | Smith | NASA |
| 39 | 04-27-90 | 1.0 | 34,000 | — | Womer | Grumman |
| 40 | 04-27-90 | 0.8 | 39,000 | — | Smith | NASA |
| 41[18] | 05-09-90 | 0.8 | 39,500 | 0.56 | Ishmael | NASA |
| 42 | 05-09-90 | 1.0 | 36,400 | 0.55 | Purifoy | USAF |
| 43[19] | 05-09-90 | 0.8 | 38,700 | 0.54 | Smith | NASA |

[1]To 22.5° AOA.

[2]To 27.5° AOA.

[3]To 30° AOA.

[4]To 35° AOA.

[5]To 40° AOA.

[6]Hoover's overall comments about this flight included: "Today's mission operation resembled the best days of the X-29A-1 flight test program." He added, "Aircraft performance to date has been extremely impressive—we definitely have a tiger by the tail here!"

[7]Purifoy's first flight on X-29A-2. It was his second flight of an X-29A, having flown as a guest pilot on the X-29A-1 program earlier; has now replaced Hoover as AFFTC X-29A Program Manager and Test Pilot.

[8]To 45° AOA.

[9]To 50° AOA.

[10]Hoover's last flight; flew X-29A aircraft 32 times; has left the Air Force and joined Northrop.

[11]Flight aborted due to sensor failure; not reflown.

[12]Ground abort due to LOX leak; flight 31 reflown on 3/29/90.

[13]Block IX-AA-01 Flight Control System software installed.

[14]Ground abort due to lack of nose gear steering.

[15]Ground abort due to LOX leak; flight 35 reflown.

[16]Previously aborted; reflown on 4/17/90.

[17]Flight aborted early; not reflown.

[18]To 52.6° AOA; first time above 50 degrees angle-of-attack.

[19]To 63.7° AOA. Aircraft wanted to continually yaw nose-left in the 53° AOA to 64° AOA region. Full right rudder pedal input was insufficient to stop the yaw-off. However, aircraft was very graceful in recovery with no abrupt movements.

Author's Note: Unfortunately, due to publication deadline, later X-29A-2 flight log data will have to be included in a subsequent printing of this volume of the Aero Series.

# Bibliography

*Aviation Week & Space Technology*. McGraw-Hill, New York, N.Y. 1984 through 1989.

Berman, Howard. "Advanced Flight Control Technology." *Horizons,* 1985; Vol. 21, No. 3. Grumman Corporation, Bethpage, New York.

Gunston, Bill. *Grumman X-29*. Aeolus Publishing Limited, Vista, California. 1985.

*Jane's All the World's Aircraft*. McGraw-Hill, New York, N.Y. 1986.

McCabe, John. "Fighters of the Future." *Horizons,* 1983; Vol. 19, No. 3. Grumman Corporation, Bethpage, New York.

Mebes, William. "Two X-29s Probing New Tactical Frontiers." *Horizons,* 1987; Vol. 23, No. 2. Grumman Corporation, Bethpage, N.Y.

Miller, Jay. *The X-Planes*. Aerofax, Inc., Arlington, Texas. 1988.

Pace, Steve. "X-29: The Shape of Wings to Come." *Airpower,* May, 1986; Vol. 16, No. 3. Sentry Books, Granada Hills, California.

Roemer, Robert. "X-29 Advanced Technology Demonstrator." *Horizons,* 1983; Vol. 19, No. 1. Grumman Corporation, Bethpage, N.Y.

*X-29 Advanced Technology Demonstrator*. Grumman Corporation, Bethpage, New York.

# Index

North American X-15, 43
Northrop, 6, 8, 33, 35
nose strake, 30, 32

**P**

pilots and personnel, 14, 41,
    55-66, 69-70
powerplants, 1, 9, 33-34
Product Development Center
    (PDC), xiii
Purifoy, Dana D., 60, 63
Putnam, Terry, 46

**R**

relaxed static stability, 30, 31
reverse airflow, 19, 24
Riemer, Jeffrey R., 60, 62, 64-65
Rockwell, 3, 6-8
roll rate, 58
rollout, 14

**S**

Sabrebat, 6-8
safety, 67
Schneider, Edward T., 60, 61
Schroeder, Kurt C., 14, 41, 43,
    55-56
Sefic, Walter, 46
Sewell, Charles A., 14, 15, 37-41,
    55-56
SFW/F-16, 4
simulations, 35
Skurla, George M., 14
Smith, Rogers, 41, 43, 48, 50, 52,
    57-58
Smolka, James W., 60, 61
Spacht, Glenn L., 10-12, 41
specifications, 36
spin chute testing, 50-53
stability, vi, 30, 31, 59
Stealth Fighter, 33
strake flaps, 24, 29-30, 35
structural divergence, 2
supercritical wing, 27
supersonic flight, vi, xiii, 42, 44
swing-wing, variable geometry, 12

**T**

T-38A chase plane, 54
takeoff, 38, 50
taxi tests, 15-17
telemetry, 35
thin supercritical wing section,
    22-23, 27, 42

three-surface pitch control, 24, 30,
    31
total in-flight simulator (TIFS), 35
transonic flight, xiii, 2
Trippensee, Gary, 44, 46, 52
Tsibin, V.P., 3

**U**

United States Air Force (USAF),
    xiii, 41-43, 47, 67

**V**

variable camber device, 23-24, 28
Voyager 2, 2

**W**

Walker, Harry C., vii, 41, 43
weapon systems, vi, 1
Wierzbanowski, Theodore, 14, 41,
    58
wind tunnel tests, 13
wind-up turns, 59
wing covers, 22, 26
wing design, 27
Womer, Rod, 43, 48, 52, 56

**X**

X-15, 43
X-29A, 5, 8
    aeroelastic tailoring in, 22, 26
    angle of attack, xiv, 25, 47, 48,
        53, 67
    approach, 40
    automated telemetry system
        (ATS), 35
    banking, 53
    canards, 23, 24, 28, 29
    climb rate, 58
    close-coupled variable-incidence
        canards (see canards)
    color schemes, 35
    composite wing box, 26
    configuration, 35
    construction begins, 14
    contractor evaluation flights
        (CEF), 14, 37-41
    demonstrator built, 14
    development of, 12-14
    developmental highlights, 9-17
    digital fly-by-wire (DFBW), 30,
        32, 33
    dimensions, 21
    fighters vs., 59
    flight logs, 73-82

    flight testing, xiv, 37-54
    forward-swept wings, 19-22
    FSW technology demonstrator,
        20
    fuel cells, 35
    functional check flight (FCF),
        50-51
    Government Phase One, 41-42
    Government Phase Two, 42-44
    inflight refueling simulation, 46
    landing, 39, 40, 51
    Mach number achieved, 59
    manual camber control, 59
    nose strake, 30, 32
    performance highlights, 42
    Phase One: technology, 13
    Phase Two: design, fabrication,
        test, 14
    pilots, 14, 41, 55-66, 69-70
    powerplants, 33-34
    program development, v-vii, xiii
    program/project
        directors/managers, 71
    records set by, xiv
    relaxed static stability, 30, 31
    reverse airflow over, 24
    roll rate, 58
    rollout, 14
    safety of, xiv, 67
    serial numbers, 14
    simulations, 35
    specifications, 36
    spin chute testing, 50-53
    stability, 59
    strake flaps, 24, 29-30
    supersonic flight, 42, 44
    takeoff, 38, 50
    taxi tests, 15-17
    technologies integrated in, 34-35
    tests, 35
    thin supercritical wing section,
        22-23
    three-surface pitch control, 24,
        30, 31
    variable camber device, 23-24,
        28
    wind tunnel model, 13
    wind-up turns, 59
    wing covers, 22, 26
    wing design, 22, 27
X-FSW Sabrebat, 6-8

**Y**

YF-17, 33, 34